TOWN & VILLAGE DISCOVERY TRAILS

The Peak District

Norman James & Abigail Bristow

Published by Sigma Leisure – an imprint of
Sigma Press, 1 South Oak Lane, Wilmslow, Cheshire SK9 6AR, England.

British Library Cataloguing in Publication Data
A CIP record for this book is available from the British Library.

ISBN: 1-85058-478-8

Typesetting and Design by: Sigma Press, Wilmslow, Cheshire.

Cover Design: MFP Design & Print

Cover Photograph: Peak National Park boundary marker on the Macclesfield to Buxton Road *(Graham Beech)*

Photographs: the authors *(except for p.65: Graham Beech)*

Maps: MFP Design & Print

Printed by: MFP Design & Print

Contents

Location Map

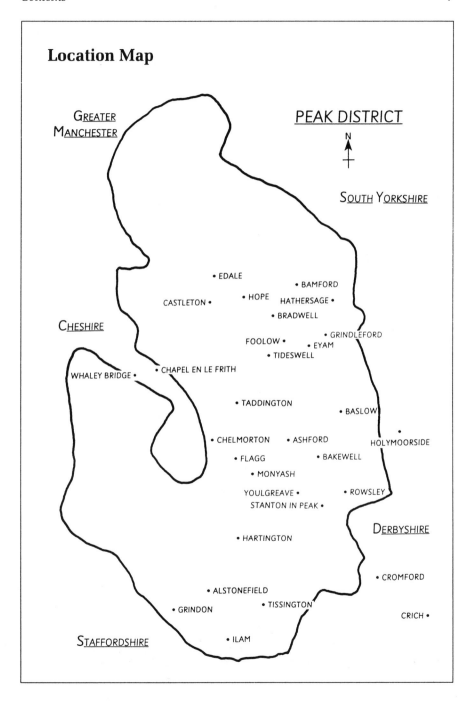

Spoilt for choice: street sign in Hathersage

Introduction

I t is difficult to know where to begin in writing an introduction to a book about the Peak District – an area which is familiar, at least by repute, to most people. This book is focussed not on the countryside that has entranced so many over the years but on the towns and villages of the area. Thirty towns and villages are featured and, for each, a walk is described to take in points of interest. The walks vary in length, though none is more than a few miles; some are very short because some villages are tiny. However, when the village trail is complete, the countryside awaits.

The trails are spread throughout the Peak District. They feature towns and villages within both the White Peak, where the surrounding rock is limestone, and also in the Dark Peak area, where the prevailing rock type is millstone grit. The different types of rock can be seen in

Edale: a mecca for walkers

the construction of both buildings and drystone walls. A great contrast is evident between these two rock types which have greatly influenced the social infrastructure within their areas.

The Peak District does not just cover a large part of Derbyshire, but also takes in parts of Cheshire, South Yorkshire and Staffordshire. The Staffordshire area of the Peak is a remote, inaccessible, and relatively unvisited area, and we have therefore taken the opportunity to include two trails within this area.

The towns and villages vary considerably in size from market towns to tiny hamlets, each with its own unique social history reflected within its streets and buildings. In some towns the walk may take an hour or two and the attractions easily occupy a day. In some of the very small villages, the walk itself may be very short, but the beauties of the surrounding countryside are an additional attraction. The description of each walk makes it clear what type of walk it is; each description also points out attractions to visit during or after the walk both in the town or village featured, and nearby.

These walks are designed to keep the walker on paved roads and footpaths; so no special footwear is required, just a comfortable walking shoe. If you want to go walking further afield, taking advantage of the dense network of local footpaths throughout the Peak, read the sections in the text under the "Nearby Attractions" heading.

The Peak District

The Peak District National Park is one the most visited attractions in the UK; well over 20 million people enjoy its charms each year. It is easily accessible from such major population centres as Manchester, Sheffield, Nottingham, etc. The sheer volume of visitors means that it is sometimes difficult to get away from the crowds; however, by visiting off-season a more peaceful experience can be achieved, if this is what you prefer. When planning a trip to "honey pot" destinations such as Bakewell or Castleton, an off-peak visit is well worth considering. In summer, the queues to enter the Castleton caverns can keep you kicking your heels for an hour or two, but from late autumn to

Mam Tor: the "shivering mountain"

early spring you may not have to wait at all; note, however, that not all the caves are open all the year round.

Ease of access is a mixed blessing for the Peak as many of the natural attractions are under extreme pressure; for example, Mam Tor received so many walkers, eroding the path to the top, that it has been replaced by steps, all the way to the top. It is a very strange experience, walking up steps in the hillside to reach the top in order to enjoy the splendid views and wondering what it used to be like when it was just a hill, without a car park at the base, but with a Celtic tribe encamped at the summit!

Access

Access to the Peak District by public transport is generally very good; even the most remote villages have some kind of bus service, and with careful planning they can be visited using public transport. When travelling by bus or train, a more genuine impression and experience of the area is likely to be yours. Bizarrely, a third of visitors to the Peak who travel by car never leave their vehicle.

Local rail services provide links with large population centres in the area. Services which provide access to destinations featured in this book are:

Matlock – Belper – Derby service, which runs to Cromford.

Buxton – New Mills – Stockport – Manchester – Bolton service, which serves Chapel-en-le-Frith and Whaley Bridge.

Sheffield – Hope Valley – New Mills – Manchester service, which serves Grindleford, Hathersage, Bamford, Hope and Edale.

Thus, eight of our featured walks can be undertaken by rail; indeed, for locations such as Edale, rail provides by far the best access. These towns and villages are also accessible by bus, as are the others featured. A few of the smaller and most remote villages have a very restricted bus service which requires careful planning – however, it is usually possible! It is worth noting that Derbyshire County Council is committed to public transport and produces an excellent timetable featuring all bus and rail services in the Peak District; the summer 1996 version was priced at 60 pence (which includes a free updating service). This is an invaluable aid to exploring the Peak District.

Telephone enquiry services include the following County Busline numbers:

Derby	01332 292200
Buxton	01298 23098
Chesterfield	01246 250450

Information on National Express Coach Services is also available from a Manchester number: 0161 228 3881.

For rail services in the area, telephone the National Railways Enquiry Line on 0345 484950.

If you choose to travel by car, parking can be difficult to find at some locations, although the problem is much reduced during the off-season. In most of the featured towns and villages public car parks are available, and the locations of the most convenient ones are given in the text of the walks. However, in some places it may be necessary to park on-street, so please remember:

¤   do not block access to houses or fields

¤   do not park on grass verges

¤   do not park on the footway

¤   try not to park directly outside houses.

Sorry if this sounds obvious advice, but all too often it is possible to see cars parked in the most inconsiderate way. In some places pub car parks are the most convenient place to park, but remember they are for patrons only; if you plan a walk before returning to the pub for refreshment, ask the landlord if you can park there. Such a request should avoid misunderstandings.

Refreshments

The vast majority of towns and villages featured within these trails have refreshments available, perhaps at the village pub or tea rooms. Reference is generally made within the text to possible refreshment sources. One of the most pleasurable aspects of these trails is to overhear the local gossip and to get a feeling for the area by visiting the tea shops and public houses.

Tourist Information

Information on local events and services is available at the Information Centres provided throughout the Peak District by the Peak National Park. The major Information Centres relevant for places visited within this book are as follows:

Bakewell (01629 813227):	Open daily
Castleton (01433 620679):	Weekend only in winter
Edale (01433 670207):	Open daily
Hartington Old Signal Box:	Limited opening

In addition to these major centres local information is freely available in many of the Peak District's rural communities mentioned within this book. The Peak National Park has set up many village information agencies in local shops and post offices; these keep the traveller supplied with information about what to see and do in the area, how to travel about by public transport, and also where to stay. Each village agency features an attractive display panel listing the above information. The locations of relevance for this book are:

Alstonefield: The Post Office and Stores

Chelmorton: The Post Office

Grindleford: The Post Office

Hathersage: The Post Office

Rowsley: The Post Office and General Store

Taddington: Mrs C Handley, Main Road, Taddington

Tideswell: The Post Office, Church Street

Youlgreave: The Post Office, Fountain Square

Alstonefield

Access

A regular bus service runs from Buxton to Alstonefield (SK131556). On Sundays during the summer, bus services from Macclesfield, Mansfield and Derby call at Alstonefield. If arriving by road, the village is located off the A515. There are two car parks in the village, one has public toilets, the other is the Community Council car park, which is free, but a donation is appreciated. When the authors visited, the first car park was overflowing, but the Community Council car park was almost empty. The latter car park has very good views over the fields and hills.

The Village

Alstonefield has an idyllic feel about it, with several successes in the Best Kept Village Competition, most recently in 1994. A village of attractive houses and gardens, with well-cared for open spaces, not so much squares as triangles of green at almost every turn. There is a welcoming air, with ample provision of seats for visitors and walkers.

Nearby Attractions

Dovedale is only a mile from the village. There are also several well-signed footpaths from the village, if a country walk is desired.

The Walk

This walk is a gentle stroll around the attractive village.

1 The starting point is the Community Council car park – however, as this is a circular walk, you can join it anywhere. Turn left on leaving the car park, at the corner, turn left past the Old Reading Room. Then bear to the right-hand side of the triangle of the green, which hosts a tree planted to commemorate a victory in the Best Kept Village competition as long age as 1966. At the next junction, bear left.

2 On reaching the attractive gift shop, turn left back onto the road through the village. This time when you reach the Old Reading Room, continue along the road. The route takes you past the other car park, public toilets and a bus stop.

3 At the next junction bear right, past Homestead Gardens, a small garden established in 1994 to commemorate the 100th anniversary

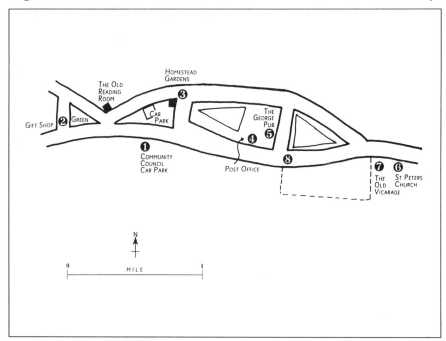

of the Parish Council. This is an attractive place to stop, especially if you have sandwiches, as there is a seat and a view across the hills.

4 Turn left onto the road and walk on past another grass triangle. The 'Post Office' is far more than a Post Office, incorporating tea rooms and restaurant, and offering accommodation, in a very pretty building. There is even a little garden opposite the main building equipped with tables and chairs for teas. This is a good place to stop if you haven't brought your own sandwiches! Above the tea rooms is a plaque recording an earlier use, J. Hambleton, Mercer and Grocer. There is an artist's studio next door.

The Old Post Office

5 Just past the Post Office is the George Pub, which has a very impressive picture of Saint George on horseback as its pub sign. The pub has gardens which almost merge with yet another grassed area with seats. Continue straight on – unless you are tempted into the pub – past the sign which records the 1994 Best Kept Village award from the Community Council of Staffordshire.

6 St Peters Church is on the right and well worth a visit. An excellent

pamphlet providing detailed information about the church is available to visitors, located near the entrance in racks. The church is a mix of designs and restorations over the years, but retains an attractive simplicity. The carved and doored pews are very attractive.

Turn left out of the church to inspect the church yard. This is a genuine village one, with grave stones dating from the 17th and 18th centuries. The pamphlet identifies the earliest memorial as that to Anne Green, dated 1518. This stone is small and round and located at the back of the church, near the rear wall – as is the grave of a woman who died in 1731, aged 107. The more recent graves stretch down the hillside, and a seat has been provided with beautiful views over Dovedale. The inscription reads "presented by the people of Alstonefield Parish Council using prize money from the Manifold Valley Agricultural Show Inter-Parish Competition Winners in 1992, 1993, and 1994". This is one of the more unusual bench inscriptions we have found. As you come round to the front of the church again notice the base of a Saxon cross. Turn left on leaving the churchyard, past the Old Vicarage.

7 At the side of the Old Vicarage is a walled and signed footpath – this is our route. This trail takes you over a few fields and stiles. If you do not wish to do this, keep to the road, retrace your steps and go to point (8). Walk along the walled path, then turn right into a field, and walk along with the fence to your left. It is easy to see the route of the path in the trodden grass. Cross the next stile and turn right, keeping the fence to your right. Go through the next stile, and over the next into a field (with an attentive pony on our visit) still keeping the fence/hedge to your right. Go over the next stile and onto the road.

8 Continue straight on past the George pub, then turn left and follow the road. Just past the car park, look for a small path, signed to the left. Follow this, which emerges in a garden, and the exit stile is to be seen on the right-hand side of the hedge. The Community Council car park is right ahead of you, and we have completed our circuit of the village. At this point it seems obvious why no houses are for sale in this village – who would ever want to leave?

Ashford in the Water

Access

A shford in the Water (SK195697) is a very attractive village nestling just off the A6, two miles west of Bakewell. It is served by a good level of bus services (full details in the Peak District Timetable) with best connections to Bakewell, Tideswell and Castleton. There is a small car park with toilets signposted in the village centre off Court Lane.

The Village

Ashford in the Water is a picturesque Peak District village which grew up around a ford on the River Wye. Its mill and lead mine were found worthy of mention in the Domesday Book. The village remained a centre of the lead mining industry until the late 19th century. A local craft industry grew up around the mining of dark limestone at Rookery Wood on the edge of the village. When polished, this stone becomes jet black (black marble) and is used as a background for coloured inkings and jewellery.

The people of Ashford pay annual homage to the abundant supply of water by 'dressing' their six wells – layering petals and other natural objects into a bed of clay to be mounted around the well; very elaborate and intricate well dressing pictures are produced. Very many visitors travel to Ashford each Trinity Sunday for the well dressings.

A view from the Sheepwash Bridge

Nearby Attractions

¤   The attractive natural feature of Monsal Head is near to Ashford and offers a choice of short, medium or long rambles in scenery of outstanding beauty.

¤   There are many attractive walks along public footpaths all around Ashford; particularly attractive paths take you to Great Longstone and Longstone Moor.

The Walk

1 The walk starts at the Sheepwash Bridge, reached from the car park by turning right along Court Lane and then left. It is reached from the bus stop by turning along Church Lane. Sheepwash Bridge is a medieval packhorse bridge, situated close to the site of the original ford. Sheep were washed in the river here before being

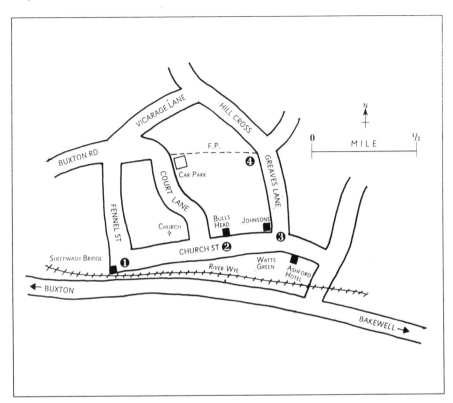

sheared. Generally the lambs were penned in on one side of the river, and their mothers were thrown in on the other side to ensure that they would get a good soaking on their swim across to their offspring. Close to Sheepwash Bridge lies the very large village well. The Cottage Tea Room offers morning coffee and afternoon teas; the Riverside Country Hotel offers teas, coffees and light bites in the conservatory.

2 From Sheepwash Bridge, walk towards the church of the Holy Trinity, passing on your left the Tithe Barn, which is of medieval construction. The church is Norman with later additions, and was rebuilt entirely in 1870. It houses relics of a local village custom, namely funeral garlands, which are suspended from the roof. They are made of paper cut into rosettes and would be carried before the coffin of a young girl in the funeral procession; the girl would have to be a virgin to qualify for this treatment. There are currently four garlands hanging in the church, the oldest dating from the middle of the 18th century. Turn left along Church Street from the church passing several cottages of note including one dating from 1899. You pass the Bulls Head public house to your left. A lane on your right, Watts Green, leads you down to an attractive view of the River Wye.

3 At the end of Church Street stands Johnsons Fine Food Store to your left, where you can stock up on some interesting and unusual provisions. Just to the right is the Ashford Hotel, where you can eat and drink in pleasant surroundings. Turn left at the food store along Greaves Lane; you pass two fine village wells on your right. There are attractive views on the right towards Monsal Head.

4 Take the footpath to the left between the churchyard and the recreation ground. This affords fine views of the surrounding hills before returning you to the back of the car park. Walk straight on here along Court Lane as far as the Peace Memorial which boasts a bench in the middle of a circular display which forms a mini-roundabout. Turn left down Fennel Street and you return to Sheepwash Bridge, where you can contemplate the Wye for a while before deciding which of the fine hostelries or tea rooms to visit for refreshment.

Bakewell

Access

Bakewell (SK217685) is accessible by bus from most areas in the Peak, which makes it an attractive base for a holiday. It is also served by express services from Manchester, Nottingham, Derby.

Bakewell is located on the A6, north of Matlock; arriving from this direction there is on-street parking slightly out of the centre opposite the playing fields.

The Town

Bakewell is an extremely attractive old market town, with pretty riverside walks, a church with great views and, of course, the ubiquitous Bakewell pudding. Bakewell has extremely good bus links with the more remote and isolated peak villages (many featured in this book), and this makes it a good base from which to explore the area by public transport. The National Park and Tourist Information Centre has a wide range of useful leaflets and books about the area to make planning excursions easy.

The town has a wide range of shops, pubs and restaurants. To return to the Bakewell puddings, these are, indeed, very different from the mass produced versions, and well worth trying from one of the two rival "original" pudding shops!

Nearby Attractions

Public transport links make most Peak District attractions easily accessible from Bakewell.

Looking back at Bakewell from the churchyard

The Walk

1 The walk begins at the Rutland Arms Hotel, easily reached by walking in along the A6 from Matlock if you have parked out of town. The war memorial is located opposite the Hotel; follow the road around, past the Bath Gardens and the Red Lion. The road now takes you past the "Old Original Bakewell Pudding Shop", and you are now on Bridge Street. The next point of interest, if you are seeking further information about the area, is the National Park and Tourist Information Centre. Follow the road past The Wheatsheaf, The Queens Arms, The Castle Inn and Scotties Bistro – there is no shortage of refreshment opportunities in Bakewell!

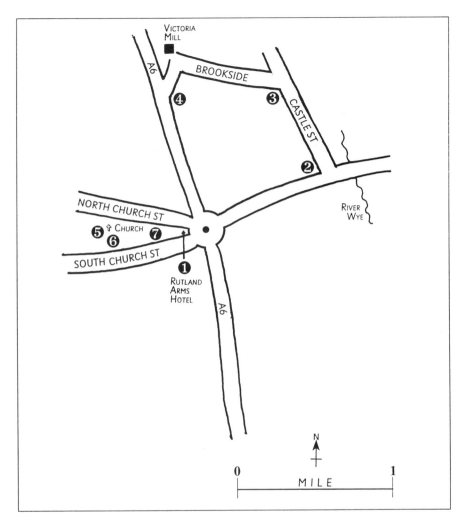

2 The road now reaches the River Wye, worth a look to admire the ducks, before turning back a little and going down Castle Street.

3 On reaching a very sweet little stone bridge, turn left along a path by the side of Milford Stream – this path is extremely quiet and peaceful. It leads you to the Victoria Mill, which the stream was constructed to serve; at this point the water disappears underground. A huge water wheel can be seen in the yard.

4 Turn left and follow the Buxton Road, back towards the town centre. Pass the Catholic church and Atkins Wine Bar and Bistro, then turn right up North Church Street.

5 Enter the church yard of Bakewell Parish Church of All Saints. This offers lovely views down into Bakewell and beyond – you can also see the remains of an old stone cross from the early 9th century. As you enter the church note the sun dial attached to the door. The vicars of the parish are listed back to Henry De Lexington, who took up the position in 1253. Parts of the church are extremely old, with Anglo-Saxon and Norman fragments. There is a lovely alabaster memorial to Sir Godfrey Foljambe and his wife, carved in 1385, and according to Pevsner, a very rare example of a medieval wall monument. Incidentally, Pevsner devotes several pages to this strange mixture of a church.

6 Exit the church yard into South Church Street, on the opposite side from North Church Street by which you entered. Stroll down the road past the Old House Museum, home of the Bakewell and District Historical Society; this museum is open on summer afternoons, and gives the opportunity to learn more about the area.

7 Continue down the road past the Jacobean Almshouses, down King Street, and find yourself back in Rutland Square; time, perhaps, to make use one of the many and varied refreshment facilities offered by Bakewell, a look around the shops or a last glimpse of the river.

Bamford

Access

Bamford (SK208836) is in the heart of the Dark Peak, half a mile north of the A625 on the A6013, and seven miles west of Sheffield. Bamford station lies to the south of the village close to the junction with the A625. Bamford is served by trains on the Hope Valley line; rail service details from British Rail on 0345 484950. Bus service details are available in the Peak District Timetable; there are regular services to Castleton and Sheffield.

There is no car park in the village, but there is limited on-street parking within the village. Please be mindful of the needs of local residents.

The Village

Bamford is a linear village snaking north – south for one mile. In former times Bamford was both an agricultural and local industrial community; nowadays, agriculture is still in evidence within the village, but the local industries of corn grinding and cotton production have died out. The cotton mill came to be owned by the Moores family, who were also responsible for the construction of many of the workers' houses in the village in addition to a church, a school and a parsonage. The parish of Bamford also covers many miles of wild and wonderful moorland above the village. The coming of the railway in the shape of the Hope Valley line opened up the area for housing, industry and commerce. Bamford now acts as a major dormitory for Sheffield.

Striding out over Bamford Moor

Refreshments

Food and drink are both obtainable in the Derwent Hotel and other public houses within the village of Bamford. Closer to Bamford station lies the Marquis of Granby Hotel, on the junction of the A625 and the A6013. Meals and refreshments are also obtainable here.

Nearby Attractions

¤ Ladybower Reservoir is within the Parish of Bamford, a couple of miles to the north-east of the village. There are opportunities here for walking in attractive settings.

¤ Bamford Moor and Bamford Edge lie high above the village of Bamford. It is possible to walk from the centre of Bamford up to a footpath which leads past Bamford Edge into the heart of Bamford Moor. The views up here are stunning: the scenery is very attractive and there are unusual flora to be observed. Attractive birds can be glimpsed catching the thermals high up on the moors here. If you wish to reach Bamford Moor by car, take the A6013 north out of the village for half a mile and then turn right on to a minor road; after three-quarters of a mile you reach the beginning of the footpath to Bamford Moor and Edge – there is limited space here for car parking. If you continue along this road after your walk on the moor, you arrive at the historic village of Hathersage, which is the subject of a further village trail within this book.

¤ There are several footpaths leading from Bamford to the surrounding countryside. Particular walks of note lead to Thornhill and Win Hill.

The Walk

1 The walk starts from the Derwent Hotel (SK208834) which serves Wards ales, and provides accommodation. There is car parking adjacent to the hotel for patrons only. Walk south towards the railway station and you find the parish church of St John the Baptist which boasts a very fine and tall steeple. Make your way back towards the Derwent Hotel, enjoying the fine views of Bamford Edge.

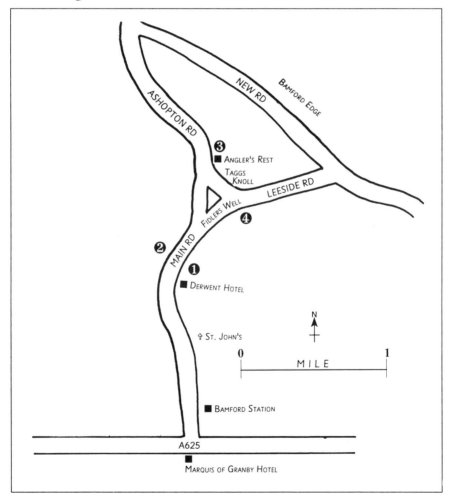

2 You may want to visit the fruit store opposite the Derwent Hotel which also sells fine baked goods. Make your way further north along the main street, passing the dental surgery with the wonderfully ornate frontage and the quaint stone Post Office. You pass a number of fine stone cottages to your left before reaching the Bamford Institute, and then the Catholic church on the brow of the hill.

3 Make your way back down the Main Street until you come to the Anglers Rest Public House, which is a fine place to enjoy a pint of Marstons, just beyond the attractive village water trough. Take the turning to the left between the Anglers Rest and the Bamford Methodist church, built between 1821 and 1889. Bear round this road, Taggs Knoll, until you meet Fidler's Well. If you turn left here and continue straight on for one mile, you come to the edge of Bamford Moor, where you can take the footpath over this desolate and secret place.

4 For this trail, however, turn right and walk back towards the centre of Bamford. You come to the attractive village square, lined with trees and benches, where you can tarry awhile. Back at the main street, turn left past Peak Fruits, and you soon find yourself back at the Derwent Hotel where you can revitalise yourself with their range of food and drink!

Baslow

Access

Baslow (SK252724) can be reached by express bus from Manchester, Stockport, Chesterfield, Buxton and Bakewell. Baslow is very well-provided with bus services and is accessible from a wide range of smaller places.

The A623 and A619 pass straight through the village. There are two possible parking places: the first is directly outside the church, where there are spaces marked on the road with a two-hour time limit; the second is the main car-park, again just off the main road at Goose Green.

The Village

Baslow is an attractive village in the midst of the Peak. It once provided a retreat for those living in the nearby cities of Sheffield and Chesterfield, providing clean air. The Hydropathic Hotel was built to meet these demands, but sadly is no more, though the gate posts remain.

Baslow is well-provided with hotels, restaurants, pubs and tea shops, located on the A619, so whatever kind of food or drink you require can probably be found.

Nearby Attractions

The obvious local attraction is Chatsworth, which helps to explain the high traffic flows at the roundabout in the village. There is a convenient footpath from Goose Green to Chatsworth.

Baslow by the riverside

The Walk

The walk is written to start from the church, but can be picked up at any point.

1 The parish church is a good starting point for the walk, and the churchyard is very attractive, looking especially good on the day the authors visited in April, with daffodils and buttercups in full bloom. The church overlooks the River Derwent and an attractive stone bridge dating from 1603. Take a look inside the church – it is almost as broad as it is long, with attractive stained glass windows and lovely floral displays for Easter. On your left as you enter is a table with guide boards so you can find your way round the sights within the church. When we visited there was also a useful, short guide to Baslow on sale at the table.

On leaving the church, continue through the graveyard along a path lined with roses and out onto the main road again.

2 Turn up School Lane, passing the Wesleyan Methodist Sunday School dating from 1822 on the left and the local school to the right. Further up this lane on your left is the Alma, a strange-looking residence that was once a public house complete with a tower; the large sign means that you can't really miss it.

3 Follow Eaton Hill as it curves away to the right, past the old site of the Hydropathic Hotel built in 1881, but demolished long ago. Are those its old gate posts? Continue along the narrow road, lined with attractive houses and gardens and down the hill onto the main road.

4 Goose Green is on the other side of the road, with the Devonshire Arms Hotel on one side and a car park, complete with public toilets on the other. There is a small local hall next to the car park which sometimes hosts exhibitions or sales. At the rear of the Green lie the Goose Green Tea Rooms, which look very inviting. Just past the tea rooms, a bridge takes you over Bar Brook; it is here that the path to Chatsworth is signed to the right, past the pretty thatched cottages.

5 For this walk, we return to the main road and turn left past the Cavendish Hotel and the sports ground. At the roundabout follow the road straight ahead, which continues through the village.

6 Walk on past the Prince of Wales. Note how the pub is almost completely surrounded by the graveyard of the parish church, with the more recent graves on the roundabout side of the pub and the older graves on the church side.

7 The road also takes you past a baker's shop and The Barn house – a coffee and tea shop, if you are in need of refreshment. Pass the church again, but this time you could take the path through the gate beside the churchyard and down to the river. There is a seat

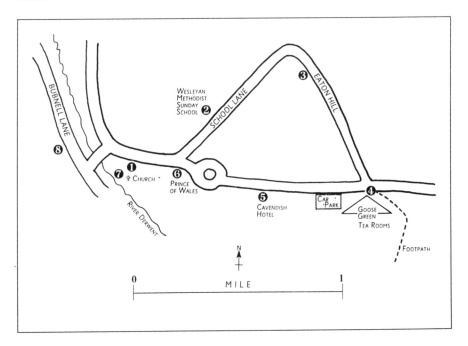

here and a very good view of the river – the ducks are very inquisitive, but really only interested in food!

8 After this diversion, stroll up Bubnell Lane, taking you over the lovely old bridge and climbing above Baslow along the line of the river. This takes you past the weir, where water was diverted to power Baslow Mill. Turn back when you feel you have had enough of the walk and the views and return to the centre of Baslow.

However, if you want a longer walk, continue along the lane which becomes very narrow and passes through very attractive hilly farmland. As the road is extremely narrow and winding, motorised traffic is infrequent and slow moving, which makes it a pleasant lane for a walk. At the end of the lane, turn right onto the B road leading to Calver, and then right again at the traffic lights onto the main A623. This takes you back to Baslow (or retrace your steps returning along Bubnell Lane if you wish to avoid the traffic). This route takes you past the Bridge Inn serving Kimberley Ales and food.

Bradwell

Access

Bradwell (SK174812) is served by regular bus services to Castleton, Sheffield, Tideswell and Bakewell; full details are contained within the Peak District Timetable produced by Derbyshire County Council. Alternatively you can call the County Busline on 01332 292200.

Bradwell is 1.5 miles south of the A625, one mile south-east of Hope, and four miles east of Castleton on the B6049. There is limited on-street parking available within the village.

The Village

The village of Bradwell is very much a working village. This trail offers you the opportunity to walk its quaint winding streets and to discover some of the history behind its fine buildings. Bradwell's prosperity was founded upon the 18th and 19th century lead mining industry, like so many of the villages within the Peak. The village soon developed other trades and industries, and it became a local centre for silk and cotton weaving; as a result, milliners' and hatters' premises sprang up, and at one time Bradwell could boast a total of seven hatters, which all used lead products!

Bradwell was the site of many battles throughout the ages: the Saxon King Edwin was reputedly killed after one such battle and hanged from a tree – this incident has lent its name to the Eden Tree, described in the walk. A local author, Seth Evans, wrote of the village thus in 1912, and it is not possible to improve on his words: "Its steep winding streets, if streets they can be called – and all sorts of queer little out-of-the-way places running in and out in all directions, break-neck, skew-tilted, beginning everywhere, leading nowhere...". His book, Bradwell Ancient and Modern, is well worth a read. Walk the streets of this village and you understand exactly what he was writing about.

Nearby Attractions

¤   Bradwell Moor, Bradwell Edge and Bradwell Dale all lie close to the village of Bradwell and each deserves a visit: quiet, beautiful places offering opportunities for peaceful rambles with spectacular views and scenery.

¤   Bagshaw Cavern, open to visitors by arrangement, is sited close to Bradwell. It is a large series of underground caves containing a variety of stalactites and stalagmites, including the Dog Tooth stalagmites which curl upwards from the cave floor.

The village of Bradwell, nestling below the moors

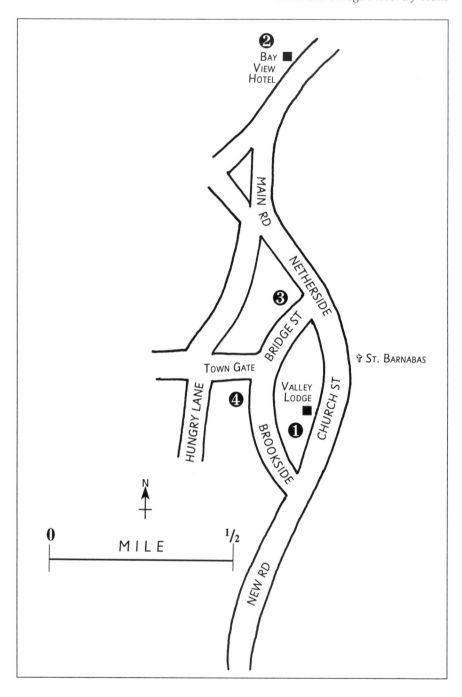

The Walk

1 The walk begins at the Valley Lodge Hotel on Church Street; this is a very fine hotel, often a winner of CAMRA awards, which offers a friendly welcome, a comfortable environment, a choice of fine ales, and a large menu (SK174810). There is parking at the Valley Lodge for patrons only. From the Valley Lodge turn left along Church Street until you reach the parish church of St Barnabas to your right. St Barnabas is an imposing edifice; walk around the churchyard to see how the village clusters within the narrow gorge, and how this has worked the quaint and unusual pattern of the streets. Opposite St Barnabas stands the Wesleyan Sunday School dating from 1844.

2 Continue along Church Street; you soon pass the Newburgh Hall Social Club to your right – this is not an attractive building, but performs an important social function within this working village. Walk past the green and you reach the Bay View Hotel and the scene of the famous Eden Tree (see above).

3 Retrace your steps past the attractive stone memorial hall dating from 1925, and the baker's shop. Duck to your right down Bridge Street, which soon becomes Town Gate. There are several buildings of interest along this quaint street: most notably, the miniature bookmaker's shop and the White Hart public house on your right. Continue along Town Gate and you soon reach Hungry Lane, a pleasant patch of green with an old cabinet maker's premises.

4 Walk back down Town Gate and turn right into Brookside. Here you can admire the pleasant recreation ground with the attractive brook flowing alongside. Pause to look at the little bridge over the brook. When you get to the end of Brookside, turn left along Church Street and you soon find yourself back at the Valley Lodge; this is a good opportunity to enjoy some refreshment!

Castleton

Access

Castleton (SK150829) is on the A625, six miles east of Chapel-en-le-Frith. The A625 used to snake around Mam Tor but, due to geological instability, the hill was threatening to engulf the road and the latter is now, literally, severed. Access to Castleton from the west – for light road traffic only – is through the truly marvellous Winnats Pass; steady nerves are needed for driving through Winnats, especially if there is snow on the ground. There are car parks signposted within the town of Castleton, and it is strongly advised that you park there; attempting to park on-street in Castleton may hold up the considerable traffic flows, as well as disadvantaging the local residents.

A better alternative for travel to Castleton is by public transport. There are bus connections to and from Castleton from most major centres within the Peak and the surrounding area. Regular services also operate from Ashford, Bakewell, Hope, Manchester and Sheffield. Full details are in the Peak District Timetable, and you can call the County Busline on 01298 23098.

The Town

Castleton is one of the prettiest towns within the Peak District. There are more buildings of note, features of interest and spectacular scenery than other any town or village within the Peak area. The authors must declare their prejudice and declare that Castleton is their favourite Peak District town. Unfortunately, they are not alone and throughout the tourist season from Easter to the end of October, the streets of Castleton and the various natural attractions can become very busy indeed. You are well advised to visit out of season when you find that you have the village streets and the myriad natural attractions more or less to yourself; what could be more fascinating, for example, than a personal boat trip through the Speedwell Cavern? Two illustrious previous tourists to Castleton were Queen Victoria and Lord Byron – presumably they did not visit the town together.

Castleton has been described as the "most educational of all English landscapes", and it is certainly true that there are things here to tempt the cultural palate of even the most jaded visitor: a Norman castle, four show caves, wonderful scenery, minerals including the famous Blue John which is mined and worked here, and the very streets, hills and dales of Castleton which are steeped in history. Castleton is situated at the western end of the broad Hope Valley; the hills are so close together here that the roads have to climb 1300 feet to leave the valley. The Derbyshire limestone ends on the shoulder of Mam Tor; north of this point are shales and gritstone. This junction of two rock types has left many interesting mineral veins within the rock, which led to the rise of a significant lead mining industry. Blue John stone is mined in Treak Cliff Hill at Castleton, and is worked into beautiful jewellery and objets d'art. Blue John is found nowhere else in the world, and you can buy some very fine Blue John works in and around Castleton; be warned, however, that the rarity of the

Speedwell Cavern, on Winnat's Pass

commodity ensures a high price!

The population of this small town is now about 750 persons, who generally are commuters, quarrymen, or earn their living from the tourist trade. Not so long ago many industries thrived within the area, making the town of Castleton totally self-contained: farming, milling, lead mining, rope making, lime burning and other rural pursuits. Remnants of many of these previous pursuits can be found as you wander the lanes and by-ways in and surrounding Castleton.

An early Celtic tribe established a fortress for itself right on the top of Mam Tor. The Romans had an encampment some three miles away at Navio, and almost certainly mined lead near Castleton. In the Norman era Peveril Castle was built, and the village was laid out in a grid pattern at its foot. Peveril Castle formed a key component of the Norman chain of defence; it was built by William Peveril, an illegitimate son of William the Conqueror.

An historic ceremony which is unique to Castleton is the Garland Ceremony, a survival of the Green Man fertility rites, which takes place on 29 May each year. The "King" wearing a large garland of flowers rides on horseback through the village, accompanied by his "Consort". The village band follows, playing the "Garland" tune, while white-clad village maidens dance to the theme. The ceremony concludes with the "King" placing the "Queen", the topmost garland, on the village War Memorial.

Nearby Attractions

There are many natural attractions within the vicinity of Castleton. In order to do the town and the surrounding area full justice, it is necessary to stay in the town for a few days. Luckily there are many bed and breakfast opportunities in and around Castleton to suit all tastes and pockets.

¤   Mam Tor is just outside the village of Castleton, overlooking Treak Cliff Hill, and attaining a height of 1700 feet. At some time in its history its steepness and shaly composition led to the slipping of a huge section, exposing the face that can be seen today. Because of its occasional subsidence and its shimmering effect, Mam Tor is known as "Shivering Mountain". The Celtic name, Mam Tor, means "mother mountain", and this name was coined by the Celtic tribe who used the summit as a hill fort some 2000 years ago.

¤ The walk to the top from Windy Knoll is strenuous and invigorating, but also most worthwhile; the views are genuinely spectacular.

¤ The Blue John Mine is situated close to the shoulder of Mam Tor, just off the A625. It is named after the famous Blue John, a mineral unique to this area which has been mined here for generations within the rich mineral seams. The visitor tour takes you through a series of high and exceptionally beautiful chambers with wonderful crystal formations, while giving some background to the mining activities. You will, of course, also see some Blue John in situ.

¤ The Treak Cliff Cavern was discovered by spar miners early this century. The outstanding features of this showcave are its stalactites and its fine deposits of Blue John mineral. Within the Dream Cave you are confronted by dozens of stalactite formations glinting in the spotlights; in Aladdin's cave the stalactite flows down the walls are pastel coloured owing to the deposits of mineral salts caused by the trickle of water. The deposits of Blue John here are truly spectacular!

¤ The Speedwell Cavern is situated at the foot of Winnats Pass and provides a unique experience for the visitor, as you are ferried underground by boat along a 'level' driven some 200 years ago by lead miners. The 'level' took eleven years to excavate in an ultimately fruitless attempt to find a rich seam of lead ore. This boat trip can be a truly unique experience out of season, when you may be the only visitor; in the tourist season you may have to queue for an hour or more to take the boat trip, as each boat can only carry 22 people, and there is only one passing point along the level. You will also be shown the Bottomless Pit, so named because the miners poured in over 40,000 tons of waste rock, but this appeared to make no appreciable difference to the depth of the pit.

¤   The Odin Mine can only be descended by experienced spelun-
    kers. It is one of the oldest mines within the Peak District, and is
    named after a Saxon God. The mine was rich in lead, and yielded
    small quantities of silver. Opposite the mine lie the spoil heaps,
    with the millstone and iron crushing ring still to be seen.

¤   The Winnats Pass, the only direct road into and out of Castleton
    to the west, is the most impressive feature of the Derbyshire
    limestone scenery. The narrow road runs through a steep, craggy
    dale, caused by the collapse of a massive underground cave
    systems. Steep grass banks rise from the 1:5 gradient, giving way
    to cliffs, ridges and pinnacles of bare white limestone. A drive, or
    a walk, through the Pass are truly memorable experiences, and
    are worth repeating!

¤   There are many wonderful and attractive walks around Castleton
    to suit all tastes and physiques. Particularly fine are the walks to
    Windy Knoll, Mam Tor and Losehill Pike.

¤   The walk along footpaths to Edale is also particularly fine.

¤   The Chestnut Centre is some five miles to the west of Castleton
    along the road to Chapel-en-le-Frith. This conservation centre is
    home to a wide variety of threatened species: there are particu-
    larly fine collections of otters, including some giant South Ameri-
    can otters, and owls.

The Walk

1 This town trail starts outside the Bulls Head Hotel in the Main
Street of Castleton. Opposite, in Castle Street, there is a small
Information Centre, where you can obtain much useful local
advice, and various leaflets and brochures. Note that this information centre opens only in the tourist season. Walk along Castle
Street, passing the parish church of St Edmund with its neat
churchyard to your left, the George public house and the attractive
youth hostel building to your right. The history of St Edmunds is
linked closely to that of the castle: begun in the 12th century, it
was known as the "Church of Peak Castle".

2 You soon arrive at the beautiful, quiet and attractive Market Place, containing the War Memorials and a tree dating from 1897 that was planted in honour of Queen Victoria. To the right of the Market Place is the entrance to Peveril Castle, which is open throughout the year. It was built by a bastard son of William the Conqueror, and its original purpose was to police the lead mining industries and the hunting within the Royal forest of the Peak. Henry II later added the keep to the castle, and visited it often. The stroll up to the castle is enervating; the views obtained and the sense of history encountered are well worth the effort. To the left of the castle entrance is the Old Barn, where you can buy souvenirs and maps, guides etc. Further left, on the corner with Bargate is Hilary Beth's tea room, where you can enjoy some local delicacies.

3 Walk a short way along Bargate, and you will see the entrance to Cave Dale signposted to the right. This is a truly delightful limestone dale, a really magical and beautiful place, which winds steeply upwards, and is above the Peak Cavern. The Dale is wonderfully hidden away behind Castle Hill, and even in the height of the tourist season, this is one of the quietest and most delightful places within Castleton, and long may it remain so! Out of season you may be the only walker in this magical dale. The entrance path leads between cottages and into a narrow cleft in the rock. Beyond this rocky entrance, the valley opens into a delightful dale with steep grassy banks and limestone cliffs overlooked by the keep of Peveril Castle. If you walk to the top of the Dale you soon arrive on the tops overlooking Castleton.

4 Retrace your steps to the Market Square, and turn to the right along Back Street. There are many beautiful stone cottages along this street, and you can also glimpse the various historic 'folds', where cottages were built around three sides of a yard. Arriving back at Cross Street, the Old Nag's Head is to your left, and further along lie various gift shops where you can buy Blue John and other souvenirs. (Note, however, that some of the best Blue John objects can also be bought at the various show caves). Opposite, on the northern side of Cross Street, there is another Blue John stone and jewellery shop, a café, and on the corner, the Ollerenshaw Collec-

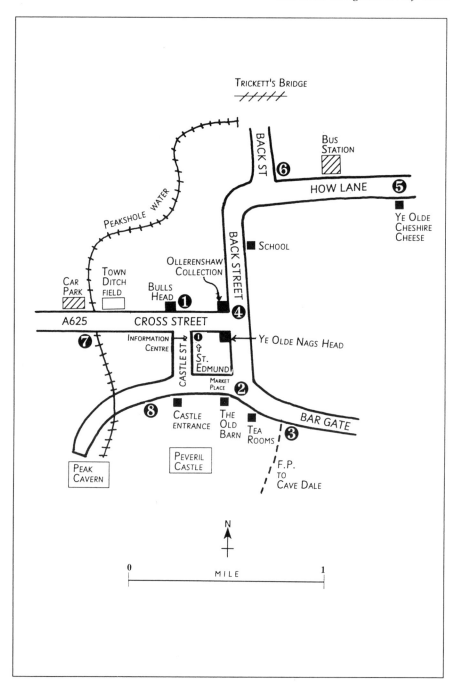

tion which houses the Blue John Museum – well worth a visit to see some truly remarkable pieces.

5 Continue along Back Street to the right of the Ollerenshaw Collection; you pass the village school and the Cinnamon Bear Coffee Shop. Bear right into How Lane with the road; on your right you pass the Peak Hotel, a residential inn serving food, and Ye Olde Cheshire Cheese with fine food and ale. Just around the corner is the Swiss House Restaurant and Hotel. Retrace your steps and you pass an antique shop, the Castleton bus station, and the Coach House village stores and Post Office.

6 At the junction with Back Lane, turn right and walk towards Tricketts Bridge, passing Mill Lane to your right where you can still see the old mill buildings. If you continue along the path beyond the bridge you eventfully arrive at Edale, having used one of the main pack horse routes which linked Castleton with surrounding areas. Make your way along the footpath to the side of Peakshole Water, accessing it just beyond Mill Lane on the opposite side of the road; this pleasant path leads you past one of the oldest parts of the village, bringing you out eventually at the car park. Town Ditch Field is by the water here; this is the remains of the town ditch which originally surrounded the whole of the fortified town of Castleton.

7 Opposite the car park, between the jewellers and the café, you can follow the signs which lead you along the Riverside walk to the entrance of the Peak Cavern. You pass many fine attractive cottages along the way, and the Dolly's China Shop and Coffee Shop. You walk to the side of the stream. The Peak Cavern has possibly the most inspiring entrance of any cave in Britain, reminiscent of the Batu Caves in Kuala Lumpur. You walk along the riverside path towards vertical limestone cliffs, before being confronted with a cave one hundred feet wide and sixty feet high. This entrance was originally used by ropemakers; some lived within the cave, and the soot stains from their fires can be seen on the roof. The show cave is a quarter of a mile long and includes huge galleries. Note that the Peak Cavern is only open during the tourist season.

8 Make your way back along the waterside from the Peak Cavern turning right at the Dolly China and Coffee Shop along the side lane which will eventually bring you back to the Market Square; from here the walk down Castle Street brings you back to the beginning of our trail by the George Hotel. Now you have to decide which of the pubs, inns or coffee shops, which are present in such an abundance within Castleton, to favour with your custom. Having once fallen under the spell of this small but fascinating town, surrounded by spectacular scenery and natural attractions, and steeped in the history of the Peak District, you will be tempted to return again and again; this is the Castleton magic at work!

Chapel-en-le-Frith

Access

Through rail services link Chapel (SK055795 is the location of the railway station, which is a little way outside the town) with Buxton, Stockport, Manchester, Bolton, and points in between. Services operate hourly outside the peak period and in the evenings. The hourly service pattern is retained on Sundays.

Chapel (SK057812) is also well served by bus services, with regular links to Whaley Bridge, Buxton, Stockport, Nottingham, Derby, Bakewell, Manchester and Chesterfield. Many of these services also serve other attractive locations in the Peak District, making Chapel a useful base for those using public transport to explore the area. There are also special services to other locations.

The A6 passes through Chapel with a partial by-pass from Buxton and Whaley Bridge, for access by car.

The Town

Chapel-en-le-Frith, also known as the Capital of the Peak and the home of Ferodo Brake Linings, means "chapel in the forest". The chapel was originally erected in the 13th century to the memory of Thomas a Beckett, then recently murdered in Canterbury Cathedral by knights loyal to King Henry II. Ferodo brake linings enter the scene later, towards the end of the 19th century, when Herbert Froode (Ferodo is an anagram of Froode!) began manufacturing brake blocks for horse-drawn wagons. Quite apart from these two claims to fame the town is a very pleasant market town, with some gruesome touches like the old stocks in the market place.

There are several pubs in Chapel offering refreshment, many serving the beers of the local Stockport brewery, Robinsons.

Nearby Attractions

Chapel is conveniently located on the edge of the Peak District, with good public transport links to other attractions. The Chestnut Centre on the Castleton Road is particularly interesting; an owl and otter sanctuary in the grounds of Ford Hall. The otters are particularly fascinating, ranging in size from the native species to a pair of giant South American otters. For further details of attractions in and around Chapel, try Mike Smith's guide to Chapel-en-le-Frith.

Otters at the Chestnut Centre

The Walk

1 Chapel-en-le-Frith railway station is some way out of town, but the walk is attractive. Follow the tree-lined lane down from the railway station; soon the vista opens out providing views of the town and the hills beyond; the lane passes under a different rail line. Turn left at the end of the lane passing under the rail line again. Turn right at the end of the road and under the rail line yet again, and on to the main street. Then turn down a road signed for car parking, Cross Street.

If arriving by road (B5470), follow the signs for parking in Station Road. The old station, ironically, is not open to passenger trains. Walk back towards the main road.

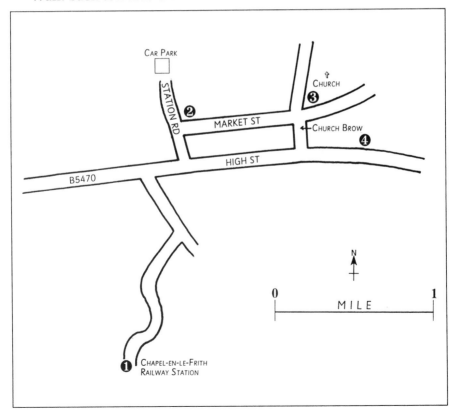

2 Turn right if following the route from the railway station, turn left if leaving the car park, down a narrow road, taking you past the Playhouse. Pass the Kings Arms Hotel and onto a tiny Market Place, with a large square War Memorial. There is also an ancient cross, and a multi-purpose trough, with levels for dogs, horses and people, now serving as a plant container. Walk on to the café with the stocks in front.

3 The church of St Thomas Becket is to the left. This is very attractive, with a sun dial over the porch; there is another sun dial in the graveyard. After visiting the church, follow the attractive winding path through the graveyard. Then exit down Church Brow, an extremely pretty and steep cobbled street with eccentric housing design.

4 Turn left onto the main street; on your left after about a hundred yards is the tiny Hearse House. This once housed the local hearse, which was rented out as required. It now houses a tourist information office, run by local people who are very welcoming; guidebooks and leaflets detailing public transport services and local attractions are available. Turn back up the High Street and return to the railway station or car park.

If travelling by car, why not visit Combs? Follow the road towards Macclesfield, and turn left to Combs Reservoir, which was very low in the dry summers of 1995 and 1996. After passing under the railway, you come to the tiny village of Combs, offering an attractive Tetleys pub, The Beehive. The interior is, unusually, decorated with chamber pots!

Chelmorton

Access

Chelmorton (SK114703) is a tiny hamlet four miles east of Buxton, one mile east off the A5270. Bus services to the village are sparse, but there are several buses a day to Buxton. Full details are contained in the Peak District Timetable produced by Derbyshire County Council; alternatively, phone the County Busline on 01298 23098. There is ample opportunity for on-street parking, but please be sensitive to the needs of residents.

The Village

Chelmorton is a tiny Peak District hamlet, relatively inaccessible in an attractive setting, which attracts few visitors. It gives the visitor an opportunity to see how a "real" rural community in the Peak still lives and works. Refreshments are available in the village pub opposite the church, The Church Inn; bed and breakfast is available here, should you wish to stay in this rural community. Chelmorton also provides a wealth of walking opportunities, as the village is criss-crossed by public footpaths.

Nearby Attractions

¤ Taddington Moor is above the village of Chelmorton, and it is

Chelmorton parish church

possible to take the footpath from the end of the High Street over the moor to Taddington; there are some spectacular views.

¤ Footpaths run in most directions around Chelmorton, but some of the most notable run to Flagg in the east, and to Back Dale and Deep Dale to the west.

The Walk

1 The walk starts and finishes in the main street of Chelmorton, aptly known as Main Street. Start at the southern end of Main Street close to the tiny Post Office, and gradually make your way to the northern end. Take the opportunity to see how the farms, which provide local employment, are integrated into the community. From the Post Office you pass the Primitive Methodist Chapel on your left dating from 1874, and once the most important focus of Chelmorton village life. The Community Hall appears on your right. You soon pass footpaths to your left to Deep Dale, and to your right to Taddington and Flagg.

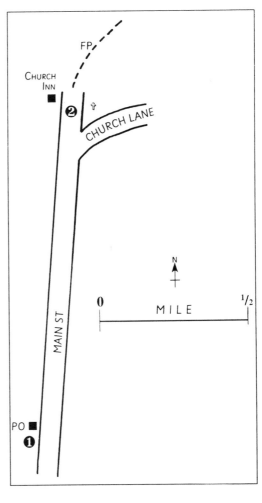

2 Continue on to the end of Main Street spurning the opportunity
to turn along Church Lane to the right. The Church Inn, a free
house, and a fine example of a Peak District village pub, stands
next to High Low Cottage, which is a very attractive building. The
Church of St John the Baptist is a true "gem". It is set at the very
end of a large village churchyard, situated on the hillside. The
church is dominated by a low tower and a high steeple. Pause a
while here to admire the church and surroundings, before crossing
to the Church Inn for refreshments. The footpath to Taddington
Moor starts at the end of Main Street beyond the church and pub.

Crich

Access

The village of Crich (SK350545) is five miles south-east of Matlock on the B5035, one mile to the east of the A6. Bus services link Crich with Belper, Ripley and Matlock and many other local communities. Full bus service details are available within the Peak District Time-table, produced by Derbyshire County Council. Alternatively, you can telephone the County Busline on 01332 292200. There is limited on-street parking within the village itself; there is a large car park at the Tramway Museum for patrons only. If you are intending to visit the Tramway Museum, and then walk within Crich, check the closing time of the Museum before leaving your car in the car park.

The Village

The village of Crich is a typical Derbyshire county village, which arose, and was sustained on, the twin industries of lead mining and quarrying. 'Crich' derives from the Roman word for 'hill'; the village is situated on a limestone mass rising to 955 feet above sea level, which has pushed up through the surrounding millstone grit, giving it a truly spectacular setting. Because of the severity of the gradients, you need to be healthy to live in Crich! While their menfolk were working in the quarry, which still stands today at the top of the village and eats still further into the hillside, the women traditionally were knitting in their own homes on machines which were hired out to them. The finished work was collected together in village ware-houses.

Crich: the tramway museum

Nearby Attractions

¤   The National Tramway Museum houses a fine collection of lovingly restored rolling stock. This, with its fine tram track snaking along the edge of the hillside adjacent to the quarry workings, is the most obvious attraction in the area; you need to devote a few hours to it.

¤   There are many walks starting within the village, and it is also possible to walk along the pleasant Cromford Canal through Crich Chase, which is just a mile or so below the village.

The Walk

1   The walk starts at the Cliff Inn public house which is on Carr Lane just to the west of the Tramway Museum. This is located in the old worked-out area of the quarry at the top of the village. Further along Carr Lane there are very fine views and walks radiating out from this quiet country lane. Walk towards the village from the Cliff Inn and you soon reach the entrance to the Tramway Museum; set aside a few hours to visit it now, or save the pleasure for later. The Tramway Museum also boasts a cafeteria and snack bar. Walk past the Museum entrance along Carr Lane; do not turn right down Cromford Road yet to go to the village, as you now visit Crich Stand, a monument to the men of the Sherwood Foresters Regiment who died in the First World War. This monument stands out for many miles from its wonderfully elevated position and is reached via a track signposted and leading uphill from Carr Lane; there is a small entry charge to the Stand.

2   Make your way back to Cromford Road, and start to walk downhill into the village of Crich. On your way to the village centre you pass some very fine examples of Derbyshire stone village cottages, particularly on your right.

You soon come to the parish church of St Mary, on your left. It dates from 1135 with a Norman nave, column and font. The church probably looks much from the outside as it did in those

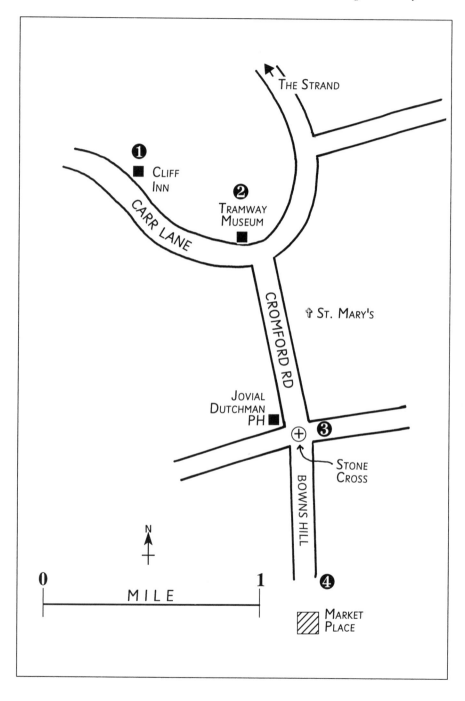

days, as it is built in the same attractive manner and with the same local materials (i.e. gritstone) as the other notable village properties. Next to the church is the village war memorial.

3 Continue to walk downhill towards the village centre. You come across an interesting stone cross in the middle of a junction; also at this junction is the Jovial Dutchman public house, named after the Dutch navvies who constructed the Cromford canal in 1794. Sheep used to be penned alongside this public house during the two annual Crich fairs.

4 Walk across this junction and continue down Bowns Hill towards the market place, which is the central focus of the village of Crich. On the way you pass the attractive Black Swan Public House to your left, and a very beautiful archway house, also to your left. On entering the village square you will find a tea room and gardens to your right, where you can refresh yourself before the steep climb back uphill to the Tramway Museum. The Baptist Chapel on the market square is a very fine building to behold. Now make your way back uphill, pausing at the hostelries for sustenance, if required.

Cromford

Access

C romford railway station (SK303574) is served by regular trains from Nottingham, Derby and Matlock. Buses also run from Derby and major towns. By car, access is off the A6 and well signed. There is a pay and display car park by the canal wharf. The canal wharf car park has toilets and a small café and shop. There is also a car park at Arkwright's Mill for those visiting the Mill.

Inside the grounds of Arkwright's Mill

Refreshments

Snacks are available at the Canal Wharf shop and inside the Arkwright Mill complex. Both are also equipped with toilets. Sandwiches can be bought from Arkwrights Off Licence and General Store.

The Old Boat Inn serves a variety of real ales; when the authors visited the selection included Bass, Cains, Old Speckled Hen and Boat Inn Bitter. It also has a relaxing beer garden, with some attractive roses – note that access to the beer garden is round the outside of the pub!

The Village

Cromford is not only an attractive village, complete with canal, river and pond, but also of importance for anyone with the slightest interest in the industrial revolution. It was here that Richard Arkwright established the first water powered cotton spinning mill in 1771, patenting the "water frame" spinning machine. This helped to open up the mechanisation of the cotton industry. The date may also explain the establishment of The Old Boat Inn in 1772. The village also features the Cromford Canal opened in 1792. Nearby are the remains of the Cromford and High Peak Railway.

Nearby Attractions

¤ If you are travelling by car, the National Stone Centre can be reached by driving through Cromford. This features panning pools outside, a display of the history of stone inside, and a shop selling stones and crystals, both polished and unpolished, and very reasonably priced jewellery. There are also very attractive views. A trail from the National Stone Centre promises train rides.

¤ A little further on along the road from the National Stone Centre you come to Middleton Top on the route of the Cromford and High Peak Railway, which was finally closed in 1967 as a victim of the Beeching cuts. The main attraction here is the Middleton

Engine which used to haul the trains up a steep incline. The route of the tracks is now a footpath and cycle trail, and cyclists are advised to dismount before attempting to descend the incline. It seems amazing now that a railway should have been routed up an incline which is now considered too steep for cyclists!

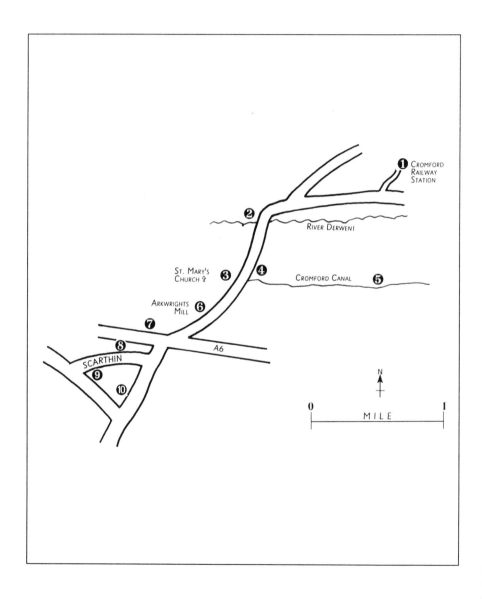

The Walk

The walk is about two miles in length, and there are so many interesting features that the duration is likely to be at least two hours – more if you stop off at the Old Boat Inn for a refreshing pint.

1 The walk begins at Cromford Railway Station, and can easily be reached from the car parks mentioned above. Descend from the railway station, at the bottom of the slope turn right onto the road signed to Cromford. This road parallels the River Derwent; the rugby club is on the opposite side of the river. Note the thatched gateway of a house on the right.

Cross to the left of the road before the bend to stay on the footway; this gives a good view of the bridge over the Derwent.

2 Return to the right-hand side of the road (again to keep on the footway) and cross the bridge. Here, the Derwent is shallow and wide but even after a very dry summer still flows quite quickly. A stone on the left-hand side of the bridge commemorates a leap made in 1697.

3 To your right is St Mary's parish church. This is kept locked, but it is worth a diversion to walk around this fine if austere building, to see the yew trees and riverbank views.

4 On leaving the church cross the road and take the path signed to the Cromford Canal. The facilities include a pay-and-display car park, toilets, snack bar and a shop selling maps, books and duck food; the ducks seem to know about this, judging by their numbers. There is also a picnic area at the side of the canal.

5 We recommend a stroll along this peaceful stretch of the Cromford Canal before returning to the road. Note the large winding hole. Walk back to the left of the shop and the canal ends abruptly; bear left at the end and you find what appears to be another branch of the canal. Return to the road.

6 Cross the road to visit Arkwright's Mill, the first water-powered cotton spinning mill, built in 1771. The mill complex had fallen into a sad state of disrepair and contamination from a period of operation as a paintworks. The complex is now owned by the Arkwright Society, who with assistance from Derbyshire County Council are slowly renovating the buildings and machinery. Although still in the process of restoration it is well worth a visit, and is well signed, providing useful information. There are also regular guided tours, priced at £2 in summer 1996. There are toilets here and a café with outside tables, also several small shops. On leaving the mill continue along the road.

7 On reaching the busy junction with the A6, bear right and use the Pelican crossing to cross the A6 safely. Then turn back to the junction (where there are public toilets) and down the road signed to Cromford.

8 Turn right just before the Market Place up Scarthin, past the interesting Old Boat Inn – well worth a diversion – this narrow road takes you up above the pond, again with ducks and occasional swans, and overlooked by the war memorial. There is also some curious but attractive street furniture in the form of wooden chairs and tables. Opposite the war memorial is Scarthin Books, which is absolutely packed with new and second-hand books. Continue past some cottages and the Primitive Methodist Chapel (1853).

9 At the bottom of the lane, turn left, past the water wheel and along the side of the pond.

10 At the end of Water Lane turn left past the antiques shop – note Arkwright's Off Licence and General Stores, opposite the junction, which offers sandwiches. Continue past the imposing Greyhound Hotel, a Theakstons Free House. Cross the A6 at the Pelican crossing and retrace your steps to the railway station or car park.

Edale

Access

The village of Edale (SK123857), really an agglomeration of five rural communities, lies in the middle of the deep valley of the River Noe within the Vale of Edale. Edale is on the Hope Valley railway line between Stockport and Sheffield, which offers spectacular scenery views as it winds through the High Peak. Road access is via a minor unnumbered road wending its way between Mam Tor and Hope on the A625. This, again, is a truly spectacular road, which can become difficult in wintry conditions. Edale station is situated at the south of the village. Car parking is well signposted, and a pay car park is sited close to the station just off the main road. There is very limited parking available within the village centre.

The Village

The Edale Valley lies at the point where the high gritstone moors give way to the shale valleys and the limestone plateau. Edale and its surrounding areas have rightly been famed as a walking area since the turn of the century. The area is also rich in social history, which has largely been shaped by its isolation, apparent in even the best of weather conditions. Until the end of the 19th century, drovers' roads provided the only means of communication with the outside world, and small paths linked the hamlets which make up the community of Edale.

The packhorse men, known as jaggers, brought cheese and salt

The Gibraltar Bridge, Edale: an important
crossing point for jaggers

from Cheshire to trade for bales of wool in Yorkshire. The packhorse bridge in Grindsbrook provided the best crossing of the Grindsbrook and the village offered the jaggers a chance to pause for refreshment before continuing their arduous journey. The true isolation of Edale can be judged by the fact that there was no church or chapel within the community until 1633; previously, worshippers had to walk to Castleton – a three-mile trek with a climb of over 600 feet.

A local corn mill provided some local employment; this was later turned into a cotton mill which provided more work. The greatest impetus to the expansion of the community, however, was the arrival of the railway in the middle of the 19th century. The population almost trebled to just under a thousand inhabitants between 1881 and 1891. Throughout the 19th century, much of the land was in the hands of the Champion family and the Duke of Devonshire, and was preserved for grouse shooting and other aristocratic pursuits. By the mid 20th century these families could no longer afford the upkeep of these extensive lands and their exclusive pursuits. The lands were sold to the Water authority, and later much of the land passed into the hands of the National Trust, which ensures that access to this beautiful and historic area is now available to all; the famous mass trespasses of the mid-20th century helped to open up this area and many other closed areas of the Peak to ordinary people. Some believe that recent legislation regarding "trespass" may turn the clock back to the days of restricted access.

The sombre moors of Kinder Scout dominate Edale, and walkers share the terrain here with a variety of animals including hares, grouse and hill sheep. The valley is so deep in the middle – well over 1200 feet – that the sun rises late and sets early even in the height of summer. Winter frosts can be very severe. The five communities which made up the original Edale community (formerly known as booths) are strung out along the southward facing slope, uphill from the previously wooded and dangerous (because of the wolves) valley floor.

The current centre of Edale, with which this trail is principally concerned, is the booth of Grindsbrook, the middle booth. Stone dominated within the booths as building material, and the fields of either side of the valley are contained within high stone walls stretching up the valley side until the land becomes too infertile or too difficult to cultivate. At this point the cultivated fields give way to meadow or pastureland, later to bracken and heather moor, and lastly to the millstone grit edging Kinder Scout.

Nearby Attractions

¤ The Pennine Way, which passes through the village of Edale, and the sombre and awe-inspiring Kinder Scout provide wonderful walking opportunities around Edale. Full details of walks in the area can be obtained in the Fieldhead Information Centre in Edale which is open daily (Tel: 01433 670207).

¤ Mam Tor, the Shivering Mountain, is on the southern side of the Edale valley; there is a car park at Windy Knoll, after which there is a short ascent by foot to the top of Mam Tor. You are rewarded by stunning views on all sides over the Peak District and beyond. Mam Tor is 1695 feet high. At some stage in its history its steepness and shaley composition caused a huge section to slip away, leaving the rough face that we see today. A local Celtic tribe used its summit as a hill fort some 2000 years ago.

¤   There are footpaths in all directions from Edale; guidebooks can
be bought within the Fieldhead Information Centre. Some of the
pleasanter and less strenuous walks lead to Hollins Cross, Barber
Booth and Nether Booth.

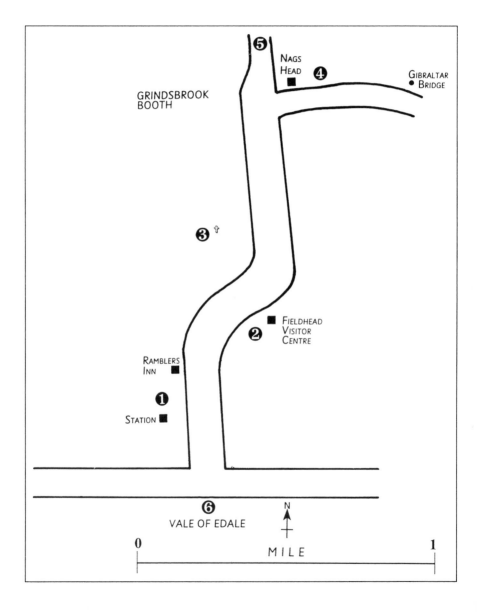

The Walk

1 The walk starts at the railway station of Edale (SK123854); the bus stop is opposite the station exit. The pay car park, the best one to use for this trail, is just at the junction with the main road to and from Hope and Castleton. On leaving the station, passing a café on your exit, turn left (northwards) along the main street to the heart of Grindsbrook. You soon pass the fine Ramblers Inn to your left which provides good ale and bed and breakfast accommodation.

2 The Fieldhead Visitor Centre soon appears to your right. Here you can learn some of the history of this area and the Peak District in general, and obtain any number of walking guides and souvenirs, as well as advice on walking from the experts. A ranger service and rescue post is also provided here. On leaving the Visitor Centre, continue to walk towards the centre of the village. Walk past the attractive Church Cottage to your left, formerly the Church Inn. The graveyard to your right marks the site of the former chapel, the first in Edale dating from 1633.

3 The current church of the Holy and Undivided Trinity is just a little farther on to your left. This very austere building also encompasses the War Memorial of Edale. Continue to walk through this wonderful village, which gives you a good view of a typical rural and isolated community within the Peak. You will see the village Post Office, set off from the main road to your left.

4 You reach the Old Nags Head, a fine public house where you can pause and recharge your batteries as you think fit. Having passed the village primary school to your right, turn to the right past the front of the pub, a 16th century coaching inn. Descend to the Packhorse Bridge over the Grindsbrook, known locally as the Gibraltar Bridge. This marks the intersection of former important packhorse routes. If you continue along the path here, you can make a fine walk to Ollerbrook.

5 Return to the Nags Head and turn right. Now you are on the way to Edale Moor, Kinder Scout and the Pennine Way and you should follow all waymarkers carefully: firstly to safeguard the privacy of local residents who generally put up with the influx of visitors to their rural community with a cheerful acceptance, and secondly to ensure that you follow the most current path; alignments may be changed to protect the paths and tracks hereabouts from erosion caused by excessive numbers of walkers.

6 When you have walked as far as you wish onto the moorlands, retrace your steps through the village to the station, pausing at the pubs and shops for refreshment as required. When you reach the end of the main street, cross over the main Hope/Castleton road to enjoy the fine views over to Mam Tor and Losehill at the southern end of the valley. If there is little traffic you can appreciate the serenity and isolation of this setting; you can perhaps get an insight into the hard life and short days of this rural community before communications opened up the Edale Valley, although even today the valley retains a wonderful individual identity and sense of "apartness".

Eyam

Access

Eyam (SK216767) has excellent public transport links to Sheffield, Manchester and Buxton using local bus services.

The A623 passes close to the village of Eyam, which is signed off it. There is a car park up Hawkhill Road; this side road is located near the road to Foolow, not far from Eyam Hall.

Stocks near the centre of Eyam village

Refreshments

Eyam has several attractive-looking pubs, among them the Miners Arms dating from 1630 – a Wards pub tucked quietly away down Water Lane. Also, look out for the Bulls Head, a Youngers Free House, known in former times as the Talbot Inn.

The Village

Eyam is famous for the behaviour of its inhabitants during the great plague of 1665-6. Once they realised the infection had reached the village from London, the decision was made to go into quarantine, to isolate themselves to avoid spreading the plague further. This was a courageous decision, as the villagers must have known that their own lives were placed at risk by staying put in an area where the plague was known to be prevalent. The village now can be read – almost literally, as many houses have plaques listing those who lived and died inside them during the plague – as a testament to their courage.

The Walk

This walk is a comfortable stroll round the village, pointing out locations of interest and options for longer walks.

1 Starting from the car park in Hawkhill Road, the museum is directly opposite if you wish to start your tour of Eyam there. It is worth noting that there are public toilets at this car park – useful information for those arriving by bus. If you turn right on leaving the car park, the road leads you to Mompesson's Well, named after the vicar who led the village through its ordeal. This was one of the points at which supplies were dropped off for the villagers to collect during the period of isolation. However, the village is to the left and we are headed for the village, so turn left down the hill, and left again at the bottom.

2 A small green complete with stocks lies to the right, offering good

views of the surrounding countryside, also a display map giving some historical information about the village.

3 The road takes you past Eyam Hall, and then some drinking troughs for animals; these form part of a public water supply system dating from 1588, which is one of the oldest in the country. There are other such troughs on this walk.

4 Plague Cottage, the cottage where plague first broke out in Eyam, is soon reached on the left-hand side of the road. The plaque attached to the building tells the story. Look out for similar plaques attached to other old buildings which tell their history regarding the plague very effectively.

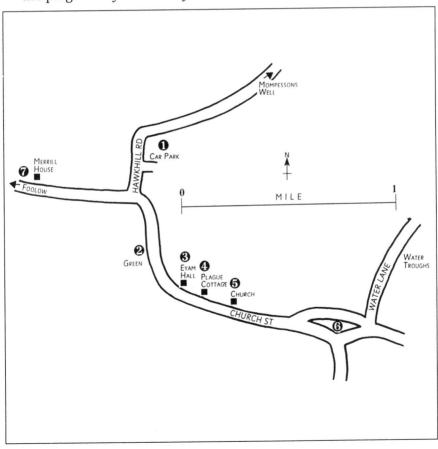

5   The church is soon reached, the graveyard featuring an 8th century
    Celtic cross; also the grave of Catherine Mompesson, the wife of
    the vicar, who stayed with her husband through the quarantine
    period, but did not survive it. There is an unusual sundial attached
    to the wall of the church, featuring the place names of many exotic
    places, some with religious connotations, others not.

    The church is very attractive inside, with aged murals at the top
    of the walls. There is a very informative display, giving details of
    the church and the history of the plague in Eyam. The information
    boards contain sad details such as the text of William Mompes-
    son's letter to his children telling of the death of their mother. An
    inventory of the belongings of a deceased woman includes an
    allowance of 5 shillings (25p) for "anything thats forgot". Other
    features include the plague register and an alpine Madonna
    perched above it. A footpath through the churchyard offers an-
    other route to Mompessons Well. On leaving the churchyard
    continue down Church Street past the Bulls Head and a bus stop.

6   The square is soon reached, with Eyam Tea Rooms at one end. An
    old bull ring is set into the pavement. Take Water Lane off to the
    left, past the Miners Arms. This lane leads you to two more
    troughs, again forming part of the old public water system; one has
    hard water for drinking, another off to the side and by a gate
    provides soft water for washing. Walk a little further up this lane
    to a bench with views over Eyam and across the countryside.

7   Retrace your steps down Water Lane and back up Church Street.
    This time, before you reach Hawkhill Road turn left along the road
    to Foolow, passing the Royal Oak pub. An interesting history lies
    behind Merril House. Andrew Merril left the village during the
    plague; he did not break the quarantine but went to live alone in
    the countryside until it was all over – he survived. A little further
    on is the house where the poet Richard Furness was born in 1791.
    Turn back towards Eyam, and the end of the walk.

Flagg

Access

Flagg (SK139684) is a small hamlet lying 5.5 miles south-east of Buxton, 1.5 miles east of the A515. On-street parking is possible within the village, but please be sensitive to the needs of local farmers. Bus services to and from Flagg are quite limited, but there are regular weekday connections to Buxton and Monyash, and school day connections to Bakewell; careful planning is required, so ensure that you have a copy of the Peak District Timetable, produced by Derbyshire County Council.

The Village

Flagg is a tiny hamlet in a natural bowl which gives splendid views on all sides. There is often an opportunity to observe some spectacular skyscapes; the accompanying cloud formations that scud by seem to put on a special show for the few inhabitants of this village. Flagg is derived from the word for sod or turf, suggesting that turf-cutting was once a major activity within the village. A high point of village life occurs on Easter Tuesday, with the Flagg Point to Point races which attract competitors and spectators from miles around. Quarrying and lead mining were formerly important sources of local employment; nowadays the only local work activity is related to agricultural pursuits.

Nearby Attractions

There are many pleasant footpaths in and around the village of Flagg, including trails to Flagg Moor. The High Peak Trail lies just on the other side of the A515.

The Walk

1 The walk starts at Flagg's tiny parish church at the north end of the village; the church is most notable for its diminutive size. From here head southwards, passing successively the tiny Post Office and General Stores to your left, and the Nursery School and 1839 Methodist Chapel to your right.

2 You shortly arrive at the gateway leading to Flagg Hall Farm, mentioned in the Domesday Book as Flagg Hall. It is believed that the Fynneys who inhabited this hall for over 400 years were descendants of John de Finnes, one of William the Conqueror's barons, who was rewarded for sterling

The parish church at Flagg

service with the title of Warden of the Cinque Ports in 1086. There is a skull in the hall attributed with mysterious powers; it is believed that if it is ever removed from the hall "strange and untoward events will occur"!

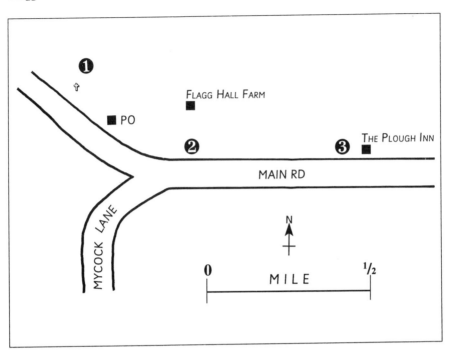

3 A short walk further along the road brings you to the Plough Public House, the social focus of the Flagg community, where you can pause to refresh your batteries after your arduous meander through the village. Just beyond the public house is the village pond. Flagg has always been supplied with water from local wells; before the coming of mains water supply, the Flagg wells were never known to fail; they served not only the local community but also neighbouring farmsteads for miles around, who came to collect water for their own needs and for livestock when their own supplies failed. Flagg is only a tiny hamlet, but a stroll through the village does give you the opportunity to look at the life of a small Peak District rural community, and to imagine how little things have changed over the years. The setting of the village allows you to appreciate how the rural life cycle is effectively ruled by nature.

Foolow

Access

The small village of Foolow (SK191768) is two miles west of the
plague village of Eyam, and half a mile north of the A623 just west
of Middleton Dale. A regular bus service links Foolow with Sheffield
and Buxton, stopping *en route* at many places of interest within the
Peak. Full service details are contained within the Peak District
Timetable; County Busline on 01298 23098 can also supply bus
times. There is on-street parking around the green within Foolow
itself.

The Village

Foolow had its heyday at the height of the lead mining boom;
nowadays, it is a quiet, friendly village of some 125 inhabitants. The
name is variously described as meaning either "multi-coloured hill",
or "burial ground" or even "hill of birds". Much of the village dates
from the 18th and 19th centuries: the Manor House and the Old Hall
are two particularly fine residences to look out for. The pond and
green, with the medieval cross reputedly dating from the 14th century, are the focal point of the village. Until the 1960s there were
about six or seven dairy herds in and around the village. These were
each collected for milking at distinct appointed times, to ensure that
there was no overcrowding at the village pond when the cattle
stopped to drink their fill. Now only one small farm remains, which
mainly farms sheep. The village is full of fine old stone farm buildings, which have now been converted into dwellings, generally for
the new locals who commute to Sheffield and elsewhere.

Nearby Attractions

¤ Sites worthy of a visit around Foolow include Longstone and Middleton Moors both with a myriad of footpaths.

¤ The wonderful country pub, the Three Stags Head, situated at Wardlow Mires. This public house, converted carefully from a 17th century farmhouse, serves a fine range of beers and has a warm welcome for all.

The Walk

1 The walk starts at the 14th century stone cross on Foolow village green; this fine cross was relocated to this position in 1868 having been moved from the Wesleyan Chapel. From the cross make your way to inspect the pond and the well; sometimes there is frog spawn in these aquifers.

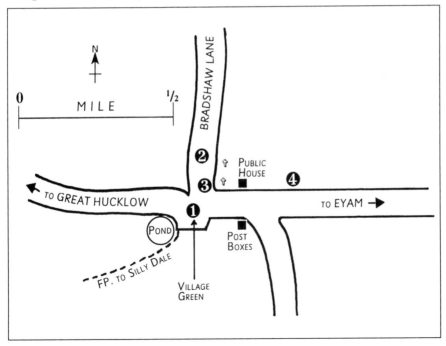

To the left of the village pond you find the beginning of a footpath to Silly Dale; this is very attractive and well worth a short jaunt. To the right of the well the road leads through the countryside to Bradwell.

2 Take instead the little lane down past the tiny Chapel of St Hugh's at Foolow. This lane leads eventually to Bretton and offers a pleasant walking environment and some superb countryside views. You may catch sight of some shaggy horses in a field to your left, opposite the alpine and rock plants nursery to your right, zealously guarded by a cat on our visit. Just beyond the city limits you come to the second village well, which features along with that by the village pond in the annual August well dressing ceremony.

3 Make your way back to the village green, and you pass the small Wesleyan Chapel dating from 1866, and the tiny church of St Hugh's. Pause to admire the fine porch on the Wesleyan Chapel, and also to examine the little building with steps to the front of St Hugh's – what is or was the function of this building?

4 Turn left at the village green and you soon find yourself at the village pub, the Bulls Head, where you can rest awhile. Once, there were five hostelries in the village of Foolow: the Spread Eagle still survives as a private house, and the Bulls Head, also known as the Lazy Landlord, is now the village pub. When you leave this fine inn, look at the fine and historic post box opposite, next to its more modern counterpart.

Foolow's historic post box

Grindleford

Access

Grindleford (SK243777) is at the junction of the B6001 and the B6521; the village is on both sides of the steeply inclined and deeply wooded Padley Gorge with the River Derwent gurgling at the bottom. Grindleford is situated 9 miles west of Sheffield; it is on the Hope Valley railway line and Sheffield is reached by train via the Totley rail tunnel, which is a truly remarkable feat of engineering, being some 3½ miles long; it was completed in 1893. Regular bus services connect Grindleford with Sheffield, Buxton, Tideswell and Bakewell; full details are in the Peak District Timetable, or you can ring the County Busline on 01332 292200. There is limited on-street parking within the village.

The Village

The name Grindleford, despite being reminiscent of a Swiss village, derives from the grindstones which were quarried locally and carried across the Derwent at the village ford. The setting of the village is truly outstanding, with the steep-sided gorge lined with a wide variety of trees, and the gently flowing Derwent in its meadows. Grindleford, despite its small population, straggles up and down hill for some two to three miles!

Nearby Attractions

Nearby points of interest include many fine walks and the National Trust properties in the immediate vicinity of Grindleford. Farther afield lie Curbar Edge and Froggatt Edge, just a couple of miles south of Grindleford.

The river meadows, Grindleford

The Walk

1 The walk starts at Grindleford railway station (SK251788) which is at Upper Padley, some one mile uphill from the centre of the village, by the bridge. Upper Padley is the destination of an annual pilgrimage for Roman Catholics who come to commemorate the Padley Martyrs, two priests who were hanged, drawn and quartered for practising their faith for the benefit of the Fitzhérbert family in Padley Hall. Sir John Fitzherbert escaped with his life but was subject to life imprisonment. Nearby Padley Chapel is the only surviving remnant of the Hall.

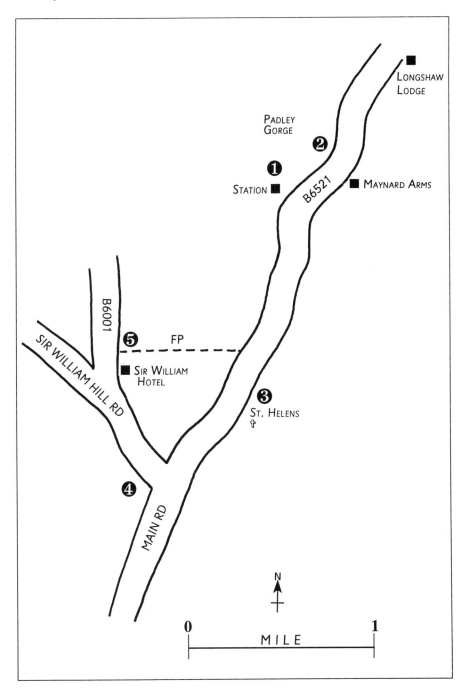

LONGSHAW LODGE

PADLEY GORGE

❷

❶

STATION ■   B6521   ■ MAYNARD ARMS

B6001

❺   FP

■ SIR WILLIAM HOTEL

SIR WILLIAM HILL RD

❸

ST. HELENS

❹

MAIN RD

N

0   1

MILE

2 Turn left up the hill and you will see the National Trust property of Padley Gorge to your left, where there are many fine walks within this attractive woodland. Continue to walk up hill as far as Longshaw Lodge – this is another National Trust property: just further downhill is Longshaw Park, again owned by the National Trust. Each of these sites is worthy of further exploration. Continue to walk downhill and you come to the Maynard Arms – a public house, hotel and a restaurant.

3 Walk down past the residential housing and you will arrive at St Helen's church; an attractive riverside walk starts from close to the church, but the walk can be muddy in wet weather. Just beyond the bridge lie the Silver Jubilee Memorial gardens and the village Post Office.

4 Turn right at the junction, uphill into Sir William Hill Road: this is a 1:7 hill! Pause to admire the fine cottage at the junction. You soon reach the Methodist Chapel to your left, with a footpath leading uphill behind it; the War Memorial stands ahead of you, and the Sir William Hotel to your right, which is listed in the Les Routiers guide.

5 Just past the Sir William, take the footpath to your right, which leads you back down to the main road along an attractive lane. Make your way back up the gorge to Grindleford station – you may decide to refresh yourself in the Maynard Arms!

Grindon

Access

Grindon (SK086544) is two miles north of Waterhouses and Winkhill off the A515. There is parking available within a small signposted car park behind and to the side of the parish church. Bus services run to Leek including a Post Bus; very careful planning is required and the Peak District Timetable is essential.

The Village

Grindon is high in the Staffordshire Moorlands, and forms part of the Staffordshire Peak District in contrast to the more accessible and busier Derbyshire Peak. It is a very isolated rural community, and is only accessible along very narrow lanes. Grindon appears in the Domesday Book as "Grendon" meaning "green hill". It overlooks the beautiful Manifold Valley, and is sited along a former packhorse route used for transporting ore from the Ecton copper mines to be smelted in the Churnett Valley. There is a public house in Grindon, but there are no shops, schools or even a post office.

Nearby attractions

¤ Given the beauty of its setting, there are many spectacular foot-paths to tempt you to ramble around the area: to Ford, to Back o' th' Brook, and to Grindon Moor.

¤ The beautiful Manifold Valley is just one mile to the east and affords many pleasant walking opportunities.

¤ You will also be able to explore Thor's Cave and Ladyside Wood.

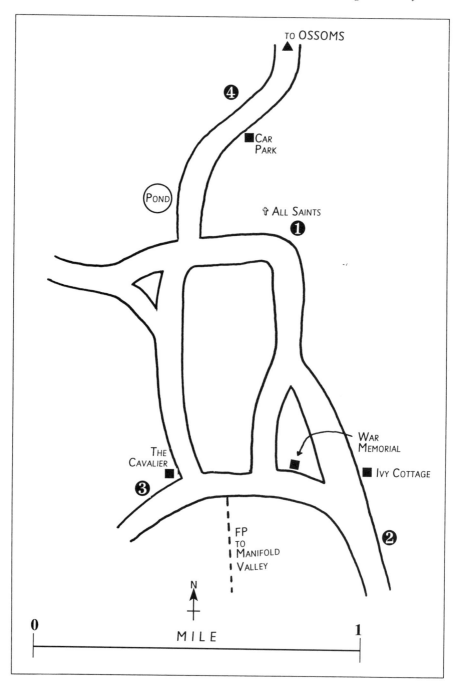

The Walk

1 The walk starts by the very austere parish church of All Saints. This has a particularly attractive churchyard, and you should note in particular the fine gargoyles, and the spectacular views from the back of the church over the Manifold Valley. Look also for the "rindle stone" to the left of the church marking a "wet weather stream" and erected by the Lord of the Manor of Grindon in 1862 to establish his right to the waters issuing from the stream.

2 Walk southwards from the church, passing the war memorial to your right. Bear left and walk past Ivy Cottage, admiring the old farmhouses and cottage gardens. When you have reached the "city limits" turn back, and this time turn left, before you reach the war memorial. A footpath leads off to the left here to the Manifold Valley. You shortly come to a quaint wooden bench, the bus shelter, and the phone box.

3 Opposite is the Cavalier Inn which offers a garden and food. Pause a while here, or continue northwards bearing to the right of the village green.

4 Continue straight on and you soon pass the village pond on your left. The road continues onwards, past the side of the church and the little village car park, forcing you up hill and down dale. Eventually, it becomes nothing more than a narrow lane, leading you to Ossoms. The walk to Ossoms is highly recommended; it affords beautiful views on all sides, as well as giving the walker some remarkable insights into the realities of rural life in such an isolated and inaccessible community. On reaching Ossoms, retrace your steps to Grindon, pausing to admire the views, the livestock contentedly munching on the pastureland, and the varied and hardy flora and fauna.

Hartington

Access

Hartington is halfway between Buxton and Ashbourne, 1.5 miles west of the A515 at map reference SK130604. A regular bus service links it with Buxton, and a less frequent service operates to Leek and Ashbourne. Full details of these services and other bus links can be found in the Peak District Timetable produced by Derbyshire County Council and available from Tourist Information Offices, or by ringing the County Busline on 01298 23098.

The Village

Hartington is a very attractive stone village lying in Dove Dale, and situated a mile west of the Tissington Trail. The attractive shops, hotels and houses nestle around the village pond and square. Walks lead out in all directions; there is public parking available in the square, and a large car park at SK128604. Conservation is important here, so take care to observe the parking signs, thereby minimising disruption to the life of the village at the busiest times. The village telephone box is painted grey to blend in with the local stone. As you stand and watch the smoke trailing gently upwards from the hotels, cottages and shops clustered around the village pond and square, you can imagine being transported back to a different time!

Nearby Attractions

¤ The Tissington Trail runs just one mile east of Hartington and affords easy and enjoyable trails and rambles along this disused railway line.

¤ Longnor is a fine market town nestling within the Staffordshire Peak and allowing a pleasant village trail and discovery tour.

¤ Hartington lies within the Dale of the River Dove, and it is possible to walk along footpaths northwards to the village of Pilsbury, following closely the line of the Dove, and return on the opposite side of the River.

The Walk

This walk provides a stroll around the village and an opportunity to see all the sites of interest before stopping for light refreshments.

1 The walk starts on the main square outside Charlie's Restaurant, Tea Room and Public House. If coming from the car park, turn left and you will arrive in the main square after 50 yards.

Walk from the village square to the large village pond, noting the pleasant Corner House Tea Room and Restaurant on your left. A short while further on you will find the spe-

Hartington parish church

cialist Olde Cheese Shop! Walk around the pond and take the opportunity to examine the fine village pump. If you take the road straight ahead, it will lead you to the village of Pilsbury along a pleasant gated road; it is possible to walk back along footpaths on either side of the Dove.

2 Take the lane between the pump and the Fleece and Tweed Shop which leads up to the church of Saint Giles. There are some very fine views over the surrounding countryside from this attractive churchyard. The foundations of the present church were laid in the early 13th century. When you enter the churchyard you can instantly see the two types of stone which have gone into the

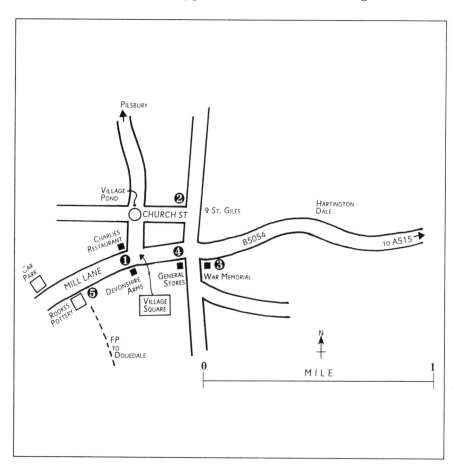

construction of St Giles – red sandstone from Staffordshire, and white Derbyshire limestone. A brief tour of the interior of this church is recommended and a small guide sheet can be bought inside the church.

3 Come out of the churchyard of St Giles, turn left, and you will find yourself at the War Memorial made up of simply-quarried stones; this is really a very moving monument. Nearby is the grey-painted telephone box referred to earlier.

4 Make your way back to the village square and you will pass in succession several interesting shops, hostelries and pubs – the tiny general stores and newsagents, the Beresford Tea Rooms, The Devonshire Arms Hotel and Public House and the Dales Craft and Gifts Shop.

5 If you walk further along to the car park, you pass public conveniences on your left; also sited here is Rookes Pottery, and the start of a footpath to take you to Dovedale, where you can enjoy some fine and leisurely strolls. Why not stay a while in Hartington? Wander around the local shops, enjoy the atmosphere and sample the delights of the local hostelries? If you wish to stay in the village, there are several guest houses and holiday cottages in addition to the hotels listed above.

Hathersage

Access

H athersage (SK232814) is an attractive stone village, nestling around its High Street, lying on the A625 6 miles east of Castleton, 10 miles west of Sheffield. The railway station provides frequent connections along the Hope Valley line – railway times are available from British Rail on 0345 484950. There are also frequent bus services, most notably to Sheffield and Castleton: service details are in the Peak District timetable. Limited on-street parking is available in the town, but there is a signposted car park.

The Village

Hathersage has four main claims to fame which are discussed in this short introduction to the village: quarrying, Robin Hood, the needle industry and Jane Eyre. It is a pleasant village sitting at the entrance to the Hope Valley, and marking the division between the Dark and White peaks of the Peak District. There are many local explanations for the name of the village, but common sense suggests that with the heather moors overlooking the village, the most likely name corruption is from "heather's edge". The name Heresiege appeared in the Domesday Book.

Settlers arrived in the area in the late middle ages, and made mill stones (querns) from the local gritstone – these were used to grind corn. The millstones produced around Hathersage were in great demand, and one enterprising local firm sent them to continental millers. Lead smelting was also once a major local industry.

Little John's grave

The Robin Hood connection is supplied by Robin's stout and hearty friend and companion, Little John, who reputedly lived in Hathersage, and is said to be buried in Hathersage churchyard. Robin himself was reputedly born at Loxley, which is only eight miles from Hathersage; many local geographic features refer to his name. Little John's cottage stood in the village until about 100 years ago. For many years a long bow belonging to Little John was kept in the parish church; it was removed for "safekeeping" about 250 years ago and has never been returned.

In the 1800s the growth of the needle industry turned Hathersage into a dirty little mill town of the dark satanic variety, mostly manufacturing needles. This does not sound particularly arduous, but the consequences could be very injurious to health, as the dust created when grinding needle points accumulated in the workers' lungs and eventually killed them.

Charlotte Bronte stayed at the vicarage in Hathersage while she was developing the idea for Jane Eyre in her mind. Many of the features and incidents within the book have their origins in Hathersage; the references to needle mills provides the most striking parallel, but the landlord of the George Hotel, a Mr Morton, may have provided the inspiration for the village of Morton in the book. The Eyre family brasses within the church may have provided inspiration for the book's name. It is possible to construct a walk around Hathersage taking in all references and potential references to Jane Eyre – this would involve a visit to the Vicarage and the Hall of Moorseats (Moor House), then along the valley to Brookfield Manor (Vale Hill) and North Lees Hall (Thornfield Hall). A very useful range of booklets about the Jane Eyre connections in th area may be bought in the parish church.

Nearby Attractions

¤ The attractive Burbage Brook nature trail is 1½ miles east of Hathersage and is well worth a visit.

¤ Hallam Moors and Redmires reservoirs are three miles north-east of Hathersage and provide an opportunity for more active rambling.

¤ There are many footpaths and quiet lanes near Hathersage itself, which reward casual strolling.

The Walk

1 The trail starts outside the attractive stone building of the George Hotel, built in the 1500s as a small inn for travellers – there is a restaurant attached. From the George, walk west along the main road to have a look at the Old School to the right. Then retrace your steps to the junction with Station Road and Mill Lane. Look out here for Bowyers, a traditional country beef and pork butcher's on the corner – not only can you buy fine butchery products, but this may be the model for the shop in Jane Eyre where the heroine attempts to exchange her gloves.

2 From Bowyers, walk towards the Little John public house, and turn right directly in front of it down Mill Lane. A pleasant walk down this lane, with the stream playing to your right, soon brings you to Barnfield Mill on your right, which was built in 1811 for the manufacture of needles. Millworkers' houses were built near the mill, so they could never really shake off their work! Walk back to the junction with Main Road, pausing to admire the fine and ornate lamp-post on the corner, which is a memorial built in 1914 to the memory of Colonel Shuttleworth. Walk east along the main Road and you pass to your left a fine series of stone cottages, the Hathersage Craft Shop and Tea Rooms, the village toilets and the village Post Office. To your right you pass Longlands Eating House and 'Outside', an excellent outdoor goods shop which also stocks a range of maps and guides.

3 Just past the Hathersage Inn, which was built by a member of the ubiquitous Shuttleworth family, turn left up Baulk Lane: you can use this attractive route to walk to the parish church of St Michael and All Angels. You will have a series of stunning views to your

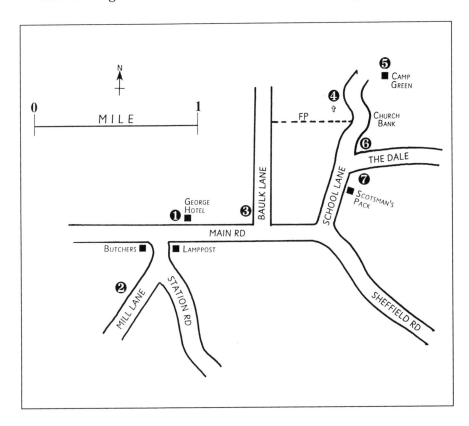

left. Take the footpath to your right, marked as part of the Shuttle-worth Memorial Walk, which takes you along the edge of pleasant fields to the parish church.

4 The church of St Michael has a long history – the present church was founded on the site in 1381, but it is believed that a Celtic missionary monk first brought Christianity to Hathersage in the 7th century, and that he might have constructed a small cell on the site of the present church. You will find Little John's grave beneath the yews in the south-west of the churchyard, although it will always be open to dispute whether it really contains the remains of robin Hood's faithful lieutenant. It is said that the grave was once opened, and a thigh bone 32 inches long was discovered – this would suggest a man of some 7 feet (2m) high. Take the opportunity to admire the fine interior of the church, and the exterior of the vicarage where Charlotte Brontë stayed.

5 To the east of the church and Church Bank is Camp Green, which dates from 850 and is said to have been built by Danes – the mound which remains may well have been originally topped by a fortification of some kind. A fine footpath is signposted leading off from Camp Green.

6 Make your way down Church Bank; when you reach the junction with School Lane and the Dale, turn left along the Dale. You soon arrive at the converted Dale Mill, which was originally powered by water from Dale Brook for the manufacture of brass buttons; it was later converted to steam, and specialised in the production of needles.

7 Walk back down School Lane, and you will soon find the Scotsman's Pack public house to your left, where you can enjoy an excellent pint with your meal. This inn is named after the pack men, travelling drapers, who sold their tweeds and cloths on this site. The village pinfold is on your right; this was used for the impounding of stray village beasts, which would be released upon payment of a fine. Back at the main road, turn right and walk back to the George Hotel through the village; take a look at Thimble Hall, a quaint cottage and shop to your right.

Holymoorside

Access

Holymoorside (SK339693) is situated just outside the Peak, three miles west of Chesterfield and three-quarters of a mile south of the A619. There is plenty of on-street parking available within the village. Bus services link Holymoorside with Chesterfield and the surrounding area – full details are contained within the Chesterfield and District Timetable produced by Derbyshire County Council; information can be obtained from the County Busline on 01246 250450.

The Village

Holymoorside is a quiet village, with most of its inhabitants now commuting to work farther afield. In earlier times there were tradesmen and craftsmen of all kinds within the local community: farmers, miners, quarriers, lead miners etc. Many of the local women were employed in Manlove's cotton mills; these large mills were prosperous for most of the latter half of the 19th century, but were then forced to close by economic necessity. They were subsequently demolished, and now hardly a trace of them remains within the village. This is a pleasant village to stroll around, and then catch up on the local gossip in one of the village locals. There are plenty of footpaths if you want to take a longer walk from the village. Some of the local gardens are truly spectacular, and some local interest is added by the River Hipper which flows through Holymoorside. The houses are built in a myriad of styles – it is up to you to judge whether they blend into a cohesive and attractive whole.

The "holy" in the village name may refer to the fact that, in the Middle Ages, monks from Beauchief Abbey near Sheffield were sent to a monastic house of correction at Harewood Grange via Holymoorside. It is more likely that the name comes from the Anglo-Saxon for hill clearing, as the heathery slopes used to come right down into the village itself before the Enclosure Acts.

Nearby Attractions

¤   Harewood Moor and Beeley Moor to the west of the village and high above it are beautiful and desolate places for walking and rambling.

¤   The attractive village of Old Brampton is to the north side of the A619 and is well worth a visit.

The rural setting of Holymoorside

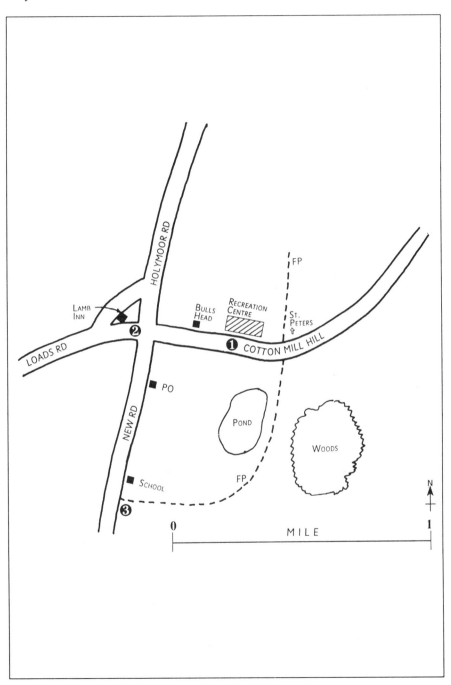

LAMB INN

HOLYMOOR RD

FP

BULLS HEAD

RECREATION CENTRE

ST. PETERS

❷

LOADS RD

❶ COTTON MILL HILL

PO

NEW RD

POND

WOODS

SCHOOL

FP

❸

N

0 MILE 1

The Walk

1 The walk starts by the recreation ground on Cotton Mill Hill just to the left of the junction with New Road. The River Hipper can be glimpsed flowing attractively alongside the road on the opposite side to the recreation ground. Walk eastwards towards the church of St Peter with its stunning graveyard setting. Just before the church is a footpath leading northwards across the fields; this provides a very pleasant stroll. If you continue along Cotton Mill Hill and follow the bend to the left, there are some very attractive views and you can enjoy some very pleasant strolls.

2 Retrace your steps to the junction with New Road, passing the recreation ground and the Bulls Head on your right. Just across the junction in Loads Road is the Lamb public house, offering an excellent place to unwind. This pub has a very pleasant beer garden. Opposite the pub are some very attractive stone cottages, and the Cottage Stores. Turn south along New Road passing the Post Office and Hendrick's Stores to your left. Very soon you pass the Methodist church and the school, built in 1874 largely financed by the mill owning Manlove family.

3 Turn left at the footpath just beyond the school on the left. This very attractive path takes you on a little nature stroll through the village where, if you are lucky, you may observe many coots, butterflies and mallards around the pond. The path takes you across a bridge over the river: a truly attractive setting. The path then takes you past the pond on your left – pause to admire the wildlife and the bulrushes. To your right is Moorlawn Coppice. The path eventually brings you out by the recreation ground. Now you only have to decide whether to take a more vigorous stroll up the hill, or to settle for refreshments in the Lamb!

Access

Hope railway station is a little out of the village, and is served by trains on the Sheffield-Manchester line, these run hourly during the week, and less frequently on Sundays.

Hope is accessible by regular bus services from the following population centres, Castleton, Bakewell, Sheffield and Chesterfield. Less frequent services link it with other places. The main services also connect Hope with attractions in the Peak District.

Hope (SK172835) is on the A625 east of Castleton. If approaching from the west, there is a car park to the right just before the centre of the village.

The Village

Hope is a very pretty village, with an attractive church and cattle market. It is a working Peak village that is also a magnet for visitors.

Nearby attractions

Castleton with its amazing selection of caverns offering sights of Blue John is only a few miles away, easily reached by bus or car.

Refreshments at the Woodbine café

The Walk

The walk is written as a circular walk from the railway station, the joining point for bus and car travellers is at (4)

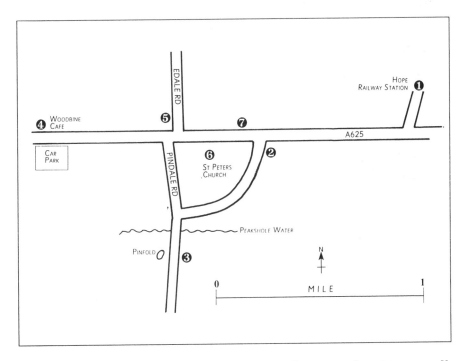

1 From the station access road turn right onto the A625, walk towards Hope, over the River Noe. Go past Daggers House with its unusual upper windows and the War Memorial to the right.

2 Turn left just before the church and follow the lane down past the old school, with its separate boys' and girls' entrances. At the end of the lane turn left and pass over the Peakshole Water. Just over the bridge there is a Pinfold, used for enclosing escaped animals until collected by their owners.

3 Turn back up Pindale Road, past the church and then left onto the main road, past the Woodruff Arms Hotel, offering Boddingtons.

4 Walk on the car park and bus stop where a public toilet is available.

The main attraction though is the Woodbine café on the other side of the road. This has a table outside – though you may have to share it with a large black cat. Food is available to eat inside or take-away: the ice creams are gorgeous, and the Eccles cakes, fresh from the oven, heavenly.

This is a good point for those arriving by car or bus to join the walk.

5   Turn back along the main road and then turn left up Edale Road. This road leads you past the Methodist church and a series of folds and courtyards. The Cheshire Cheese Inn offers refreshment. Return to the main road and cross over to the church.

6   St Peter's church is very attractive, despite the gargoyles round the south door. The churchyard features clipped yews and part of a Saxon cross.

7   On leaving the church walk on past the cattle market, worth a look if it is a market day, and then return to the station.

Ilam

Access

Ilam (SK136509) is five miles north-west of Ashbourne, three miles off the A515. Alternatively it can be reached from the A52 Ashbourne to Leek road. Bus services are generally infrequent and trips to Ilam by bus should be carefully planned using the Peak District Timetable and the County Busline on 01332 292200.

The Village

The village of Ilam is dominated by the Ilam Park Estate now owned by the National Trust. The village is one of the southernmost within the Peak and affords a most attractive appearance, thanks mainly to the efforts of Jesse Watts Russell. He was a wealthy local industrialist who had the village rebuilt in the last century including the hall, the church and the houses.

Nearby Attractions

¤ Thorpe Cloud and Thorpe Pastures are nearby local natural attractions which offer many opportunities for walking and yield spectacular views.

¤ The River Manifold is close to Ilam and offers the opportunity for many pleasant riverbank strolls

¤   Dovedale is two miles east of Ilam and offers some spectacular walking opportunities. It is generally considered to be the most beautiful of the dales in the White Peak. The name "Dove" comes from the pre-Saxon for black, and presumably refers to the dark and shadowy passage of the water through the gorge. The splendid scenery of Dovedale has delighted generations of visitors, and also inspired many literary works, including Izaak Walton's "The Compleat Angler".

Over thousands of years, the River Dove has carved out a steep-sided valley which yields swirling currents, curious rock formations and shallow cave systems. Many fascinating flora and fauna can be found throughout the length of the Dale; worthy of note are the ash woods which have been designated as an area of special scientific interest. Among the birds to be seen are herons, kingfishers, jackdaws and wagtails.

Swiss-style housing in Ilam

Dovedale now forms a key part of the National Trust's South Peak Estate and is visited by thousands of tourists at the height of the season. Bus connections are as above for Ilam; a car park is provided at the southern edge of Dovedale below Thorpe Cloud (SK148508). With careful planning it is possible to walk the three and a half miles from here to Milldale, and then catch a bus to return you most of the way to the starting point. The Peak District Timetable made available by Derbyshire County Council provides the necessary information.

The Walk

1 The walk starts at the National Trust car park (pay attendant) (SK132507) within Ilam Hall Country Park – there is limited on-street parking available within the village. The land that is now Ilam Hall and village was once part of the estate of the Benedictine Abbey at Burton on Trent. On the dissolution of the monasteries it was put into private hands by Henry VIII eventually becoming the property of Mary, wife to industrialist Jess Watts-Russell for whom it and the village were extensively rebuilt and revamped. The hall is now a Youth Hostel (not open to the public). The extensive grounds of the country park are, however, open throughout the year. There is a National Trust shop and information centre within the hall, where you can buy a guide to the gardens. In the car park look at the "Pepperpot", a small octagonal tower formerly serving as a dovecote. It is well worth having a leisurely stroll around the park as it is well stocked with an excellent mixture of mature trees. From the car park make your way down the main driveway towards the village. On leaving the estate, glance leftwards to see the fine Church of England school on a small rise, and pause to admire the attractive chalet-style village housing. The surrounding countryside reminded Jesse Watts-Russell of the Alps and he, therefore, had the houses built in this unusual, but strangely functional, style within the Peak.

2 The large cross in the centre of the village was built by Jesse on the death of his wife in her memory. You will notice that there are six water troughs around the base of the cross. There is a bench on the pavement from where you can admire the cross. Quite often the Ilam Ices van is parked here, and you can enjoy some fine local ice cream.

3 Walk on a little further to the bridge over the River Dove, and admire the attractive pasture lands on either bank of the river. You can meander a while here on the footpaths along the banks of the river.

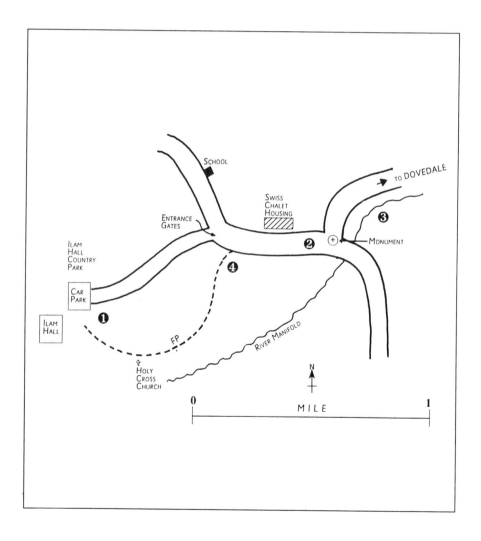

4 Retrace your steps to the estate entrance, but this time take the footpath to the left of the entrance which leads you round Dovedale House, formerly the vicarage, to the Church of the Holy Cross. The churchyard is full of unusual and attractive gravestones and memorials which are worthy of some attention. The shafts of the Saxon crosses are over 1000 years old. The first church at Ilam was built by the Saxons well before the Norman invasion; the church has been subjected to many alterations through the ages to cater for changing needs. Leave the church and continue to ascend the path which brings you back to the car park. There is a tearoom here, the Manifold Tearoom, housed within the stable block, and open throughout the year. This is a pleasant place to pause, relax and contemplate the grounds. The nearest public house, the Dog and Partridge, is back at the crossroads/junction where the attractive gated road through Thorpe Pastures departs leftwards – this is midway between Tissington and Ilam.

Monyash

Access

M onyash is in the heart of the High Peak, four miles west of
Bakewell along the B4055, and one and a half miles east of
the junction with the A515. Regular bus services connect it
with destinations throughout the Peak District – full details in the
Peak District Timetable published by Derbyshire County Council.
There is limited on-street parking in the centre of the village, but
please be sensitive to the needs of the many working farms in and
around the village.

The Village

Monyash (SK150665) is a small village within the High Peak, effectively sited within a natural bowl, and is surrounded by hills on all
sides which makes for some spectacular views of the scenery and the
skyscape. Several working farms are still present in and around the
village. The village is one of the quieter in the Peak, and its inhabitants are a true mixture of locals and incomers.

Nearby Attractions

There are many interesting and attractive footpaths leading from
Monyash, some of them taking in the various tumuli to be found in
the immediate environs of the village. Half a mile east along the road

to Bakewell, a footpath leads off to the right which takes you to the
highly attractive Lathkill Dale.

The village square at Monyash

The Walk

1 The walk starts at the main village square, where limited on-street
parking is available and the Monyash Bus Shelter proudly stands.
Pause here to admire the village cross and the war memorial. On
one side of the square is the attractive Bulls Head Public House,
and also the Old Family Tea Rooms and café, where hikers are
welcomed. On the other side of the square stands the school built
by subscription in 1871.

2 Walk east along Church Street as far as the church of St Leonard.
This pleasant, squarish, Peak-style church is worthy of a brief
inspection. Just beyond the church is the village store and tea
rooms. You can continue to walk along Church Street until you
reach the city limits, marked in Monyash usually by a gaggle of
geese in a farmyard to your right.

3 Retrace your steps to the village stores, and take the footpath to the left between the stores and the church. This path takes you on an attractive meander through the back ways of Monyash, leading you out eventually behind the village pond on Bakers Road.

4 Turn left here and you shortly come to the old parish pump, with what appears to be a pinfold behind it (a pinfold was an enclosure used the impounding of stray animals).

5 Walk back to the village square and this time walk across northwards towards the village of Flagg. You soon come to the Primitive Methodist Chapel and Monyash Community Centre to your right. Now is the time to decide whether to continue to walk along this quiet road with its spectacular views, or to return to Monyash to take advantage of its opportunities for suitable refreshment.

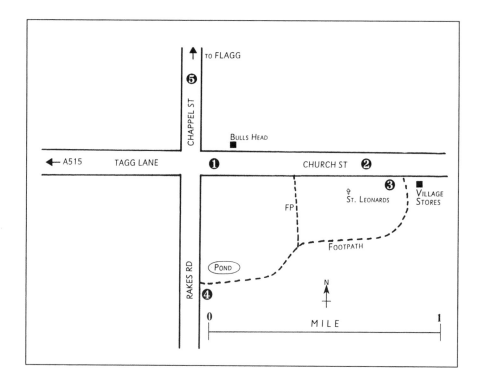

Rowsley

Access

Rowsley (SK257660) has good bus links to Nottingham, Derby, Matlock, Buxton, Bakewell, Manchester, Wirksworth and Belper. There are less frequent services to other destinations. Rowsley is located on the A6, south of Bakewell, north of Matlock. Parking is available down School Lane.

The Village

Rowsley is or was an estate village, mostly owned by the Duke of Rutland, whose Peacock symbol can be seen on the Peacock Hotel. In earlier years most residents would have worked on the Duke's Estates. The village grew on the arrival of the railway in 1849, sadly now disused. Rowsley is a small village that from the road looks like a strip development, however, there is more to it than that. The Cauldwell Mill and Craft Centre provides an interesting distraction.

Nearby attractions

The obvious local attraction is Chatsworth.

The Walk

1 From the School Lane car park, return to the main road and turn right along it. Rowsley Bridge soon carries you over the River Derwent, which is wide and attractive at this point. The Grouse and Claret offers Mansfield beers. Continue along past the bus stop (joining point for bus travellers).

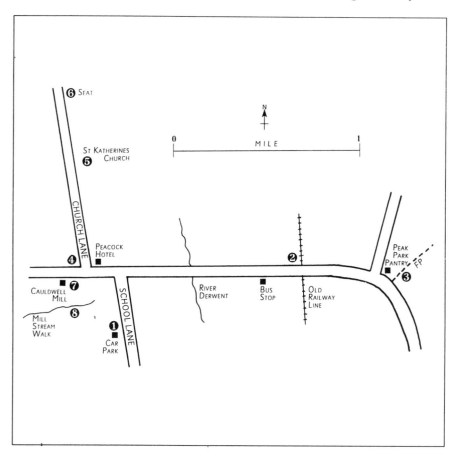

2 The road now crosses an old railway line, the old station can still be seen to the left. The line used to run through Darley Dale to Matlock. Railway cottages are on the left.

3 The road now bends round past the Peak Park Pantry on the corner. Before turning back towards Rowsley it is worth walking a little way up the footpath to the side of the shop which leads up the hill, with fine views.

4 Stroll back along the road into the village, at the Peacock Hotel, complete with stone peacock, turn left up Church Lane. Walk past a small fountain on the right and the Post Office and general store. A footpath to the right is signed to Chatsworth, offering a longer walk, perhaps for another day.

5 The road takes you up past St Katherine's church, which has an attractive Victorian graveyard, and offers lovely views to the rear of the church. An old rail viaduct can be seen to the right. At the entrance to the church yard is an unusual and attractive war memorial, with a Saxon-style cross.

6 Follow the road up a little further, and just before the edge of the village, discover a seat at the side of the road offering beautiful views down into Rowsley and across the hills.

7 Tear yourself away from the views and return down Church Lane and turn right onto the main road, to visit Cauldwell Mill and Craft Centre. The centre is based around the mill built in 1874, which utilises water from the River Wye. This is still a working flour mill and the product is for sale along with a large range of other items in the shop. There is also a cafeteria, and some small craft workshops. Ducks wander around, don't trip!

8 There is a very attractive short walk along the Mill Head Race, with its nine-foot drop. Walk along to the sluice gates and weir which link it to the River Wye; an intriguing feature here is a fish ladder to enable fish to move freely both ways. Return to the car park or bus stop.

Stanton in Peak

Access

The 170 bus service between Bakewell and Matlock calls at Stanton in Peak (SK241643), this service runs approximately hourly during the day Monday to Saturday, and at a lower frequency on Bank Holiday Mondays, but there is no Sunday service.

By road, off the A6 south of Bakewell, turn onto the B5056 and then right onto the narrow road to Stanton in Peak.

The Village

The village is very small and the walk a short one, which offers beautiful views, an attractive church and a welcoming pub.

Stanton village shop and post office

Nearby attractions

¤ The Nine Ladies stone circle is the most notable of the remains, mainly barrows and cairns on Stanton Moor and is easily accessible on foot from the village; you will need a Pathfinder map of the area.

¤ Chatsworth House is also nearby; indeed the views from Stanton, include Chatsworth.

The Walk

1 Starting from the bus stop by the pub, walk up the road to School Lane. Stroll along to the 1879 primary school and admire the open views to the left, including what amounts to an aerial view of Chatsworth. Return to the main road, past the village shop and Post Office.

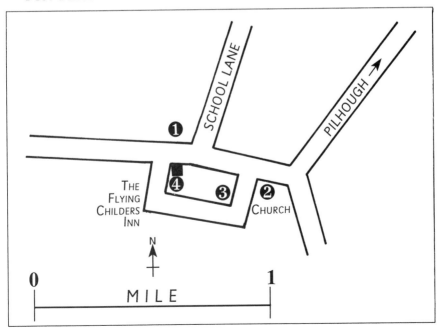

2 The church is a short way up the road on the right. This is the lovely, tiny church of Holy Trinity dating from 1839. There is an ornate stone memorial, in the style of Florentine Quattrocento, to Henry Bache Thornhill who died in 1822 at the rear beside the altar. The organ, restored in 1965, is large for the dimensions of the church. There is also a barrel organ over the door.

3 As you leave the church notice the graveyard on the opposite side of the road, down a short lane. Below the church, is the War Memorial, surrounded by trees. Turn left down the lane, past the garden of an enthusiast; this lane takes you past some very attractive houses and gardens before depositing you back on the main road by the pub.

4 The Flying Childers Inn is well worth a visit, offering Wards and Boddingtons real ales and food. This is a slightly offbeat rural inn, with a serving hatch (non-functioning on our visit) into the porch and two bars, one for bar meals, the other mainly for drinkers.

This is the end of the walk. However, if a longer walk is desired, why not take the narrow lane towards Pilhough, a walk of approximately three-quarters of a mile, giving superb views of Chatsworth. If travelling by public transport, this can be extended to Rowsley on the A6, which might enable you to return by bus, though this would need careful checking beforehand.

Taddington

Access

The village of Taddington (SK143711) is midway between Buxton and Bakewell just to the south of the main A6. Bus connections run frequently to Buxton, Bakewell, Manchester, Stockport, Matlock, Nottingham and Derby. Full details are available in the Peak District Timetable, and from Derby Busline on 01298 23098. Parking is possible on-street within the village, but please be sensitive to the needs of local residents and businesses.

The Village

Taddington is a linear village of beautiful stone cottages, which line the straggling main street. It is a quiet backwater, now that it is by-passed by the main A6. It is one of the highest villages in England, standing at over 1000 feet above sea level – it is reached along the A6 via Topley Pike from Buxton, and after a steep climb through the beautiful Taddington Dale from the direction of Bakewell. In the past the two major sources of employment were farming and leadmining; the former activity persists to this day as the village is surrounded by good pasture land used mainly for cattle and sheep farming.

Nearby Attractions

¤ A brisk walk up The Jarnett, the main road leading south of Taddington beyond Humphrey Gate opens up beautiful vistas from the crest of the hill back to Taddington and forwards to Monyash.

¤ An attractive footpath starting at the western edge of the village snakes across Taddington Moor towards the village of Chelmorton, passing a chambered cairn on the way.

¤ Many fine walks and trails possible within Taddington Dale and Monsal Dale which is adjacent. These dales can be accessed via the A6.

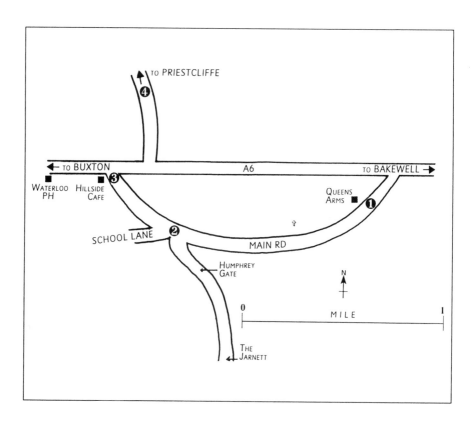

The Walk

1 The trail starts at the Queens Arms public house at the southern edge of the village; this pleasant village pub embraces much of the social life of the village. Start to walk in a northerly direction and you soon reach the War memorial, close to the entrance to the parish church of St Michael and All Angels. There is a particularly fine lych gate serving as the entrance to the dramatically large churchyard. The church is of a very attractive, and typically Peak, limestone construction; from the churchyard you can see the whole of the village, sweeping around in a semi-circle. Part of the church dates from the 12th century, and the stone font dates from the 13th century.

2 Continue to walk northwards and you soon pass Humphrey Gate to your left. There are fine views from this street which eventually becomes The Jarnett and then yields truly spectacular views. Walking past Humphrey Gate you pass the TT Road and Mountain Bikes repair shop to your left, the Village Stores and Post Office to your right.

3 After a couple of hundred yards you reach the junction with the A6 where the Hillside café stands. A walk of 300 yards further along the A6 will bring you to the Waterloo public house which effectively marks the end of Taddington.

4 Priestcliffe, though on the other side of the A6, effectively forms one community with Taddington and can also be visited for a stroll in truly rural village surroundings. The combined population of the two parishes is around 450 persons.

Tideswell

Access

Tideswell is situated seven miles east of Buxton, one mile south of the A623 (SK153758). There is parking on-street within the town, and several small car parks. Tideswell is served by an extensive network of bus services throughout the Peak District – full details are in the Peak District timetable produced by Derbyshire County Council.

The Village

Tideswell, with its church known as the Cathedral of the Peak, stands 1000 feet above sea level on the limestone plateau of the Peak. It is very much a linear village, and its attractions lie close to its main thoroughfare. Tideswell has traditionally been a prosperous market town, with its inhabitants also enjoying employment in lead mining, coal mining and agriculture. Some quarrying and agricultural employment remain, and a new light industrial estate provides local employment. Historically, there were five markets a year for cattle and local produce; the tradition has now been revived, although the markets are only held twice annually. Cattle are no longer traded here, but the Cow Club, founded in 1838 to provide insurance against cattle diseases and the ensuing veterinary expenses, is still active within the village.

Nearby Attractions

Miller's Dale, with its many opportunities for walking and rambling, is just 1½ miles to the south of the village of Tideswell. Tideswell

Dale is just south of the village and leads to Millers Dale. Monk's Dale is a mile to the west of Tideswell, and the pleasant village of Wormhill lies just further east. Every one of these attractions is worth a visit to allow a little exploration; each town and village, each dale and valley within the Peak contains its own story waiting to be discovered.

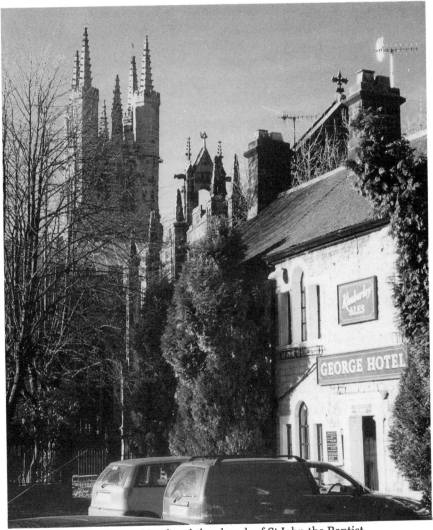

The George Hotel and the church of St John the Baptist

The Walk

1 The walk starts on the Buxton Road outside Ron Hall's family butcher, where there are some off-street parking spaces (SK152755). Follow Buxton Road northwards passing the Methodist Chapel on your left and also the attractive Coronation Cottage, with its very pleasant verandah. Pass to the left of the war memorial, and the road becomes Queen Street.

2 Turn slightly left and go straight ahead into the High Street. Walk as far as the Market Square with Bagshaw Hall on your left. There are attractive walks along Manchester Road which continues straight ahead. Retrace your steps to the junction with Queen Street, passing and admiring: the Star public house to your left; Centre Stage selling clothes, furniture and aromatherapy also to your left; the Chapel House furniture workshop to your right; and ABC, the Arts, Books and Crafts shop to your left. On your arrival back at the junction, turn left as Queen Street becomes Commercial Road. Pass Poppies Restaurant and Tea Rooms on your left, and it is worth pausing a while to enjoy the small but pleasant Bank Square Gardens, also on your left.

3 Continue along Commercial Road and you come to the "Cathedral of the Peak", the parish church of St John the Baptist, which is truly an inspiring, if sombre, edifice. You pass Tindalls on the right which serves fine pies and other foods. The church of St John the Baptist stands on the site of an 11th century chapel; the present church dates from the 14th century. Take some time to explore the interior of this fine building. From the rear of the church you will notice the old Tideswell library housed in a fine old building. Leave the church and continue leftwards along Commercial Road; you soon come to the George Hotel: here you can eat and enjoy fine ales from the Hardy Hansons brewery. Opposite the George is the Tideswell Dale Rock Shop, which stocks Blue John stone in a variety of guises, but note that this shop has very limited opening hours.

4 Take Church Lane (The Cliffe) off to your right, opposite Markowitz Ironmongery and Agricultural Suppliers. At the first bend

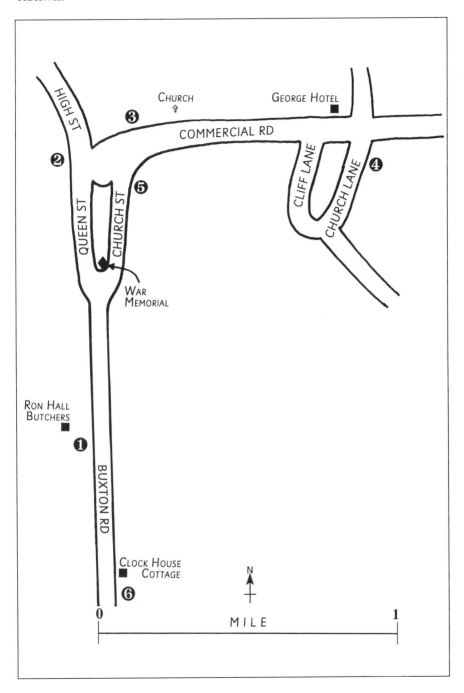

take the paved footpath to the right, which will lead you back to Commercial Road. Along the way, there are fine views and fascinating glimpses into village life just off the main street. Back at Commercial Road, turn right and head back to the George, if you are seeking further refreshment, but our trail takes us to the left.

5 Turn left into Church Street, which takes you past the village Post Office and past the other side of the War Memorial. Walk on and you reach Hills 'n' Dales Tea Shop on your left; note the limited winter opening hours. A little further along is the small Catholic church, with a very big graveyard!

6 Continue along Buxton Road until you reach Clock House Cottage to your left, where it is worth noting the donkey weather vane and the adjacent stable block. The road continues ahead to Tideswell Dale and Miller's dale. Retrace your steps, however, to the centre of the village, passing the piano showroom to your left and the fine stonework of the Hose and Jockey public house. You can now continue to discover the fascinating back street life of Tideswell for yourself – there are many attractive stone cottages to be seen, and from a variety of viewpoints the well-laid out surrounding fields above and beyond Tideswell can be clearly glimpsed.

Tissington

Access

The village is north of Ashbourne just off the A515, and the access road is signed. Surprisingly, this is a private road to the village, protected by cattle grids. The narrow and unfenced road is popular with cyclists and surrounded by grazing sheep – so drive carefully!

Follow the road past the tearooms to the Tissington Trail car park (pay and display – modestly priced). The car park has a small shop, toilets and cycle hire facilities. There is a toilet for the disabled and it is worth noting that the trail, following the path of an old railway line, is accessible to the disabled for much of its length.

Tissington (SK175525) is a very popular destination, and although the car park is large, it is advisable to arrive early, especially during the peak holiday periods.

Buses serve Tissington, mainly as shopping services for the villagers. Local buses drive right into the village, whereas the more long distance services stop at the end of the access road on the A515. A useful service for visitors is the 202 Mansfield – Derby – Ashbourne – Buxton – Castleton. In 1996, this service ran on Sundays and Bank Holidays.

The Village

Tissington is a small, extremely attractive village, with no less than six wells. A dominant feature is the Jacobean Tissington Hall, home of the Fitzherberts. Unfortunately, this magnificent looking building is not open to the public, but the outside views are well worth pausing over. The village has a popular teashop, with outside seating.

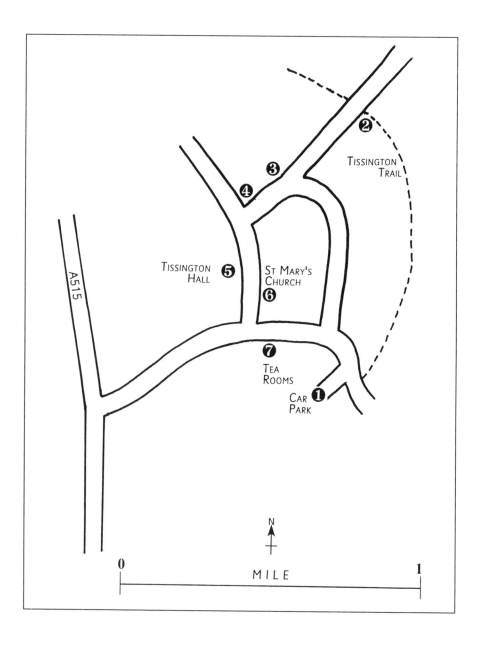

The Walk

This walk is a short circular around the village using part of the Tissington Trail and local (quiet) roads. The walk involves a short stretch of footpath which can be muddy in wet weather; an alternative route is provided for those who would rather stick to the roads. If you are interested in exploring the area further, the shop in the car park has leaflets detailing longer walks involving the Tissington Trail and local footpaths; try "Walks about Tissington".

1 Start from the car park, the opposite end from the shop, and pass under a bridge over the old railway onto the Tissington Trail. You are now on the path of the old railway, which linked Tissington with Ashbourne, a victim of the mass rail closures in the 1960s. Much work has been put into this trail to make it attractive to people, animals and plants. This section is managed by Derbyshire Wildlife Trust. Follow the well-surfaced trail, through an old cutting surrounded by trees. The cutting gradually opens out to reveal wonderful views across the peaks.

2 Just before reaching another bridge over the old railway and with a house ahead on the left, turn left up the steps signed to Tissington and Parwich. Then follow the footpath above the railway line and over the stile into the lane (this section can be muddy in wet weather).

3 Turn left into the lane, past the old farm building and continue along the lane. Where the lane forks, bear right, the first views of Tissington Hall now begin to open up to the left. The lane winds left past a house with an elongated garden and mailbox on the gate.

4 The village now appears. To your right in front of one of the houses is the first well, Hands Well, which resembles a large plant pot. Just beyond it is a craft shop. Continue to the left along the road, past the Post Office, with an entrance to the side of what looks like an ordinary house. Another small well, Childrens Well, is set into the base of a wall on the right-hand side of the road.

5 Once past a few houses, with lovely gardens, the village opens out into fields on the left, while on the right is Tissington Hall. To the left in front of the Hall is the most imposing of the village wells, Hall Well. There is also a seat with a view of the Hall.

6 Take the path to the left, to the tiny St Mary's church. A guide to the church is available inside. There is an impressive memorial to the Fitzherberts and some interesting stained glass. The most curious feature is the 11th century font, which has carvings of animals around it, including a snake – "very barbaric" is the conclusion of Pevsner! After taking a look around the church and graveyard, descend to the road again. The village green is ahead of you, with a stream running across it at surface level before disappearing below ground again on either side. The bus stop is located on the other side of this green.

7 Walk past the tea rooms – formerly a school – or indeed stop for afternoon tea! Continue past the attractive pond which accommodates the Tissington Fly Fishing Club and return towards the car park. Note Town Well to the left, resembling a dog kennel. Just before you reach the car park, along the road to the left is the final well of the village, Coffin Well. Return to the car park and your starting point for this walk; as you enter the car park, note the wired off chicken run to the right.

Alternative route (avoiding the section of footpath)

Exit the car park via the vehicle entrance, turn left when you reach the road. Then take the road almost immediately on your right, past a beech tree planted in 1934 and the small Coffin Well. This quiet and narrow lane takes you past the tiny Methodist Chapel. Follow the road until you reach a junction, turn left at the junction and continue down into the village. Pick up the original route at point (4).

Whaley Bridge

Access

Whaley bridge is on the railway line connecting Manchester with Buxton; full details of the regular train service can be obtained from Rail Enquiries on 0345 484950. Whaley also enjoys an extensive connection of bus services to the Peak District and surrounding areas; details are available from Derbyshire County Busline on 01298 23098.

The principal road connection to Whaley Bridge is the A6. Whaley lies seven miles south of Manchester and three miles north of Buxton at map reference SK011815. There are some small car parks in the town centre; this town trail starts from the canal wharf which is close to the car park, signposted off the A6 opposite the station.

The Town

Whaley Bridge is a linear town snaking along the valley of the River Goyt. It has been famous since Roman times as a crossing point of the Goyt. Its Anglo Saxon name translates as "clearing by the road", signalling a time when the Macclesfield Forest covered the whole of this area. Coal mining was the chief industry in the town until the coming of the Industrial Revolution when textile mills sprang up on both sides of the Goyt, and a corn mill was also established. The face of the town changed significantly in this period and the size of the population trebled.

Transport connections became vital, and the Peak Forest Canal was extended by an arm which linked Whaley into the canal system. The railway arrived in the 1850s and henceforth provided the key transport link. Only one mill works remains, and most traces of the coal mining industry have now disappeared. Several light industries now thrive in Whaley, which also derives income from the tourist industry with its fitting description as "Gateway to the Peak". Walkers, ramblers and other visitors travel to Whaley to enjoy the pleasant strolls and rambles possible along the canal and the Reservoir. Wherever you walk in Whaley there are clues to the past which shaped and developed the town's appearance.

The canal wharf at Whaley Bridge

Nearby Attractions

¤   Dunge Farm Gardens, three miles west of Whaley at Kettleshulme and open to the public for most of the year.

¤   The Goyt Valley, lying just beyond Whaley and offering unrivalled walks and rambles in spectacular Peak District scenery

¤   Short trails and walks using the extensive network of public footpaths to the east of Whaley.

The Walk

The walk takes you along the attractive banks of the canal, leads you back to the centre of town on side roads, and allows you to wander the fascinating High Street. There are also details of optional add-on rambles to the Toddbrook Reservoir, often compared to the scenery of Switzerland, and to the village of Taxal, three-quarters of a mile west of Whaley Bridge.

1 The starting point of the trail is the old canal wharf (SK011817), which is accessed by crossing over the A6 from outside the station and turning left downhill for 100 yards. Alternatively, the canal wharf is 50 yards to the left of the free car park signposted off the main A6. Narrow boat trips on the canal are available. Take the tow-path to the right of the canal: this is an attractive section, linking Whaley to the canal system, with the River Goyt below and to your right.

2 Continue along the tow-path until you reach the canal fork to the right which will lead you to Buxworth. Cross the footbridge and turn right along the Buxworth canal arm – you are now walking on the left of the canal. Initially you pass some very fine narrow boats which are moored here, some of them permanently. Soon, however, the canal loses its navigability, and you find yourself walking along a quiet and enjoyable backwater. The water is home to a fine collection of aquatic plants and also to families of large black and white ducks, some twice the size of mallards! Attractive cottages line the left-hand bank of the canal arm. The River Goyt now lies below you to your left, and it passes over a series of weirs.

3 You arrive at the canal basin at Buxworth – refreshments can be obtained at the Navigation Inn directly ahead. The Navigation is proudly featured in the Campaign for Real Ale Good Beer Guide and serves a fine range of good beers. Turn right at the road here and pass over the new bridge.

4 You shortly arrive at a group of cottages. Turn right by Townsend Cottage up the road marked "no vehicular access". There is a half mile steep ascent along this very quiet road, before a descent with

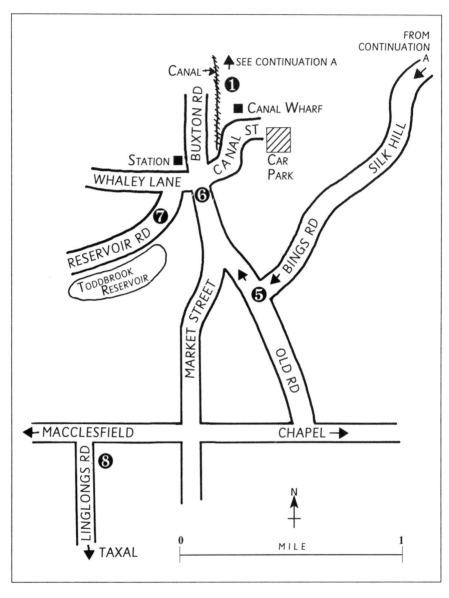

fine views which will return you to Market Street. The frog/toad crossing sign is worthy of notice. Follow down with the road all the way into Whaley, passing the now disused chapel to your right.

5 At the bottom of Bings Road, turn right and follow this road back

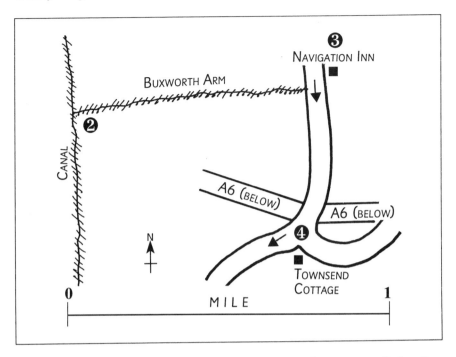

to the High Street. The name, Bings Road, is one of the few reminders of the coal mining which used to be the major economic activity in Whaley Bridge; "bings" is the old name for a mine spoil heap. Back at Market Street (A6) you can make your way back rightwards to the canal wharf, pausing to admire the number of interesting shops which line the road. Some, such as Hallam Saddlemakers to the left of the rail bridge, service the country pursuits market.

6 There are several pubs, restaurants and cafés in this part of Whaley where you can pause to recover from your exertions: the White Hart Public House, the Narrow Boat Bistro, the Navigation Inn and Simon's Bistro will all be passed on your way back to the canal wharf, or the car park. Look out also for the headquarters of the Plain English Campaign!

7 You can extend your walk by turning left before the station and going under the bridge; you then take the left fork into Reservoir Road – after a quarter of a mile you find yourself at Toddbrook

Reservoir, where you can take a leisurely and attractive stroll. The wooded slopes surrounding the reservoir are said by many to be very reminiscent of Switzerland!

8 Another excursion can be made, by walking south down the High Street to its junction with the B5470. Turn right here in the direction of Macclesfield and ascend the steep hill for half a mile. Just before the brow of the hill turn left into Linglongs Road signposted to Taxal. Another half-mile stroll down here brings you to the hamlet of Taxal, most notable for its isolated rural setting and its pleasant parish church of St James, dating from 1287, but mainly rebuilt in 1825. An unusual memorial tablet lies in this church commemorating the late Michael Heathcote "gentleman of the pantry and yeoman of the mouth". This native of Taxal went served King George II as "food taster"; his remains were returned for burial to his home village at the time of his death at the age of 75, suggesting that there could have been few attempts to poison the king! There are many attractive footpaths and country lane strolls which can be made around the hamlet of Taxal.

Youlgreave

Access

Youlgreave (SK210642) is in Bradford Dale, three miles south of Bakewell, and three miles east of Parsley Hay on the A515. A reasonable bus service connects with Bakewell and other local communities, but a bus trip to Youlgreave should be planned with care by obtaining the Peak District Timetable from Derbyshire County Council, or by phoning the County Busline on 01332 292200. There is a large free car park signed to the west of the village; on-street parking can be very fraught here, and will only annoy the local inhabitants.

The fountain in the square at Youlgreave

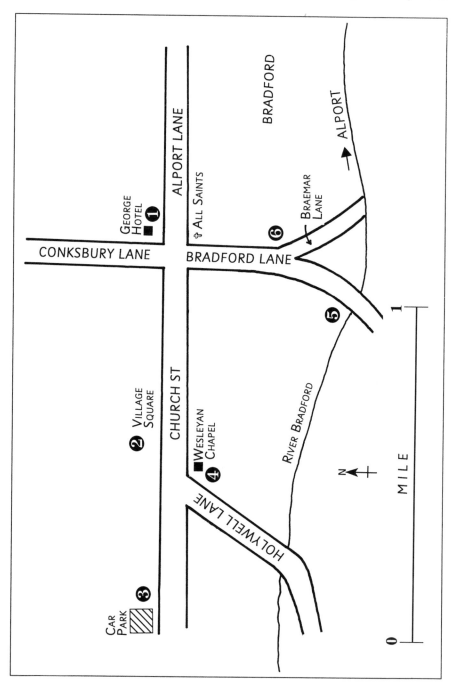

The Village

Youlgreave is a straggling, attractive Peak village set in the beautiful Bradford Dale. Youlgreave is sometimes known as Youlgrave, and the name may mean "yellow grove". The village is extremely attractive, but perhaps best visited out of season, as it can become very busy with tourists and sightseers. It is a wonderful starting point for wanders and rambles along Bradford Dale and Lathkill Dale.

Nearby Attractions

¤ Lathkill Dale is one mile to the north of Youlgreave, and provides wonderful walking and rambling territory, best accessed from Over Haddon. Alternatively you can walk along the River Bradford as far as Alport, and then turn north along the banks of the River Lathkill which bring you after a mile or so to Lathkill Dale and Over Haddon.

¤ The River Bradford offers the opportunity for many pleasant meanders; you could, for example, wander westwards along the river from Youlgreave to the village of Middleton by Youlgreave.

¤ There are several tumuli, stone circles and even a cave, accessible by footpaths to the south of Youlgreave: the Ordnance Survey Map 119 (1:50000) is perfectly adequate for following these paths.

The Walk

1 The walk starts at the George Hotel, a pleasant inn at the eastern edge of the village, which offers a warm welcome, an extensive food menu and a good range of beers. Opposite the George is the Church of All Saints with its attractive churchyard. The church is actually in Bradford, as the two villages meet at this point. From the church, walk west along Church Street into the heart of Youlgreave. You pass traditional stone shops and buildings on both sides of the street before arriving in the main village square. Pass a traditional butcher on your right, and to your left you see:

an ornate vicarage; a traditional butcher and grocer; the former Youlgreave Cooperative Society (now a Youth Hostel); and the Bulls Head, which serves food and provides bed and breakfast. The Youlgreave Cooperative was founded to help the families of the quarrymen who were often laid off for weeks at a time when the weather conditions made the quarry unworkable. Goods were made available on credit, to be repaid when better weather came and the wage packets started coming in again.

2 The village square in Youlgreave has several interesting buildings and features. The fountain in the middle dates from 1829, and underneath it is a 1500 gallon water tank; the water travelled to the fountain head via the first piped supply in the village. You also see the quaint Youlgreave Post Office in this main square, in addition to the village chippy and a gift store.

3 Go further along the street and you pass, to your right: the Farmyard Inn and the Primitive Methodist Chapel. Retrace your steps to Holywell Lane which leads off to the right, just in front of the Wesleyan Chapel.

4 Walk down Holywell Lane passing the toilets and the village hall. You soon come to the Meadows Tea Rooms, with a fine view over Bradford Dale. It is particularly pleasant to sit here in summer over a cuppa, watching the Dale below. On arrival down by the River Bradford, turn left and walk along the river bank. You pass ducks and geese as the river merrily burbles along over a series of small weirs. You can wander happily up and down stream.

5 Our trail leads you up Bradford Lane, when you meet the first main road. This lane leading uphill return you to Bradford, the church and the start of the walk at the George Hotel.

6 For a variation turn right along Braemar Lane from Bradford Lane – this leads you through a traditional limestone dale, having crossed over a pleasant bridge. You can see how traditional farming survives within the Dale. You eventually arrive in the village of Alport, and can return to Youlgreave back along the Dale, or along the quiet road.

Index

A

B

C

D

Other titles of interest from:

TEA SHOP WALKS IN THE PEAK DISTRICT

Popular walking duo **Norman and June Buckley** are quickly becoming the country's tea shop experts - **"...the shape of things to come...highly recommended"** THE CONGLETON CHRONICLE. *£6.95*

CHESHIRE WALKS WITH CHILDREN

This book from **Nick Lambert** was the first in our "Walks with Children" series and it has quickly become a firm favourite. Things to look out for and questions to answer along the way make it an entertaining read for young and old alike.

£7.95

PEAK DISTRICT MEMORIES: the photographs of E. Hector Kyme

Roger Redfern

E. Hector Kyme (1906-1987) was a renowned photographer whose work appeared in a wide range of publications. His great love was the countryside, high hills and farming life. He knew the Peak District intimately, from a lifetime of cycling and walking there. Roger Redfern, a long time friend of the photographer, has selected a representative sample of photographs taken over the last thirty years of Hector Kyme's life to form this fascinating view of the Peak District National Park and adjacent fringes. Superb photographs and entertaining text make this truly a collector's item.

£9.95

For further details of these and many more fine books, please contact:

Sigma Leisure, 1 South Oak Lane, Wilmslow, Cheshire SK9 6AR
Phone: 01625-531035; Fax: 01625-536800; E-mail: sigma.press@zetnet.co.uk
Free catalogue. ACCESS and VISA orders welcome – 24 hour Answerphone service!
Most orders are despatched on the day we receive your order – you could be enjoying our books in just a couple of days. Please add £2 p&p to all orders.